HEART HEALTHY PIZZA

*Over 100 Plant-based Recipes for the Most Nutritious Pizza
in the World*

by

Mark Sutton

ISBN-13: 978-1469981383

ISBN-10: 1469981386

Published by CreateSpace: v1.70

ACKNOWLEDGEMENTS

It's difficult to pay adequate homage and gratitude to all those who've influenced me and helped make this book a reality.

Drs. Neal Barnard, John McDougall, and Dean Ornish: your work paved the way. Robert Cohen, aka "The NotMilkMan" for your column, vision, and "SoyToy." Janet Enoch, for fostering my original idea. The Mgmt. and team at Trader Joe's in Fairfax, VA for professionalism, advice, and help during a difficult period. My far right and far left "counselors" at Giant in Gettysburg, PA, Jeff and Dennis: you lent needed ears. To my "Pizza Posse" from the Fat Free Vegan Group: Traci Brendencamp, Anthony Carriero, Debbie Cowherd, Victoria Christison, Keda Maru, Sandy Mathiesen, Lance Mateas, Shayla Smith, and Josette Thompson. As testers and proofreaders you were all superb.

Marion and Elliott, for enthusiastic and timely feedback. Valerie Wagner, an astounding tester and listener. You were incredible. Kurt and Sue Christensen: Sue's kitchen and vegetable garden were a godsend, and I wish Kurt hadn't talked me out of my "vegan sushi pizza" idea ("it's just SO wrong!"). I owe you both so much. Jim and Mo Rogers: Jim's 24/7 willingness to listen to my rants and provide advice was vital, and feedback from both of you seminal. The astoundingly prolific vegan cookbook author, Robin Robertson, for early encouragement, advice, and interchange.

Dr. Caldwell and Ann Esselstyn: for changing my life and I'm thankful. To my father and mother for incredible support on all fronts and unfettered access to their home and amazing kitchen: I can never thank you enough.

Finally, to my good friend, Howard Lyman. You were the "cut me no slack Doctorial Thesis Committee" in one man that I needed. Without your personal example, experience, guidance, patience, and insistence that this book needed to be done, it wouldn't have. You have my profound gratitude and I'm blessed to have worked with you over these many years.

This book is dedicated to everyone who wants to design and create nutritious heart healthy pizzas for living longer, feeling stronger, and loving better.

(and also, to all those people who insisted it couldn't be done!)

Table of Contents

Foreward by Howard Lyman, 3

Introduction, 5

Chapter 1: Firm Foundations, 9

The Process, 9

Tips & Techniques, 12

Basic Dough Recipes, 14

Gluten-Free Dough Recipes, 17

Chapter 2: Amazing Gracious Sauces, 23

Tips & Techniques, 23

Red Sauce Recipes, 25

Green Sauce Recipes, 30

"White" Sauce Recipes, 33

Chapter 3: No Nonsense Non-Cheese Sauces, 39

The Process, 40

Tips & Techniques, 41

Grain-Based Recipes, 46

Legume-Based Recipes, 71

Tofu-Based Recipes, 77

Vegetable-Based Recipes, 83

Chapter 4: Powerful Pizza Possibilities, 87

Tips & Techniques, 88

Old World Pizza Recipes, 89

New World Pizza Recipes, 99

Other World Pizza Recipes, 112

Resources, 125

Glossary, 133

Appendices

1: Reasons for Choosing a Plant-Based Diet, 147

2: The Problems with Added Oil or Fat, 151

3: Fat Stats for Commercial Plant-based Cheeses, 155

4: Cooking Legumes and Grains, 159

Indices

Recipes Index, 165

General Index, 169

About the Author, 179

Foreword

"As far back as I can remember pizza has been a comfort food for me. Thin crust, thick or deep dish, hot or cold, you name it, I would eat it with great delight.

I have always been interested in creative pizza. The more varied the toppings and crusts, the greater my desire in trying something new. My wife has made some of the most interesting creations in my pizza history until I met Mark. He has taken pizza making to a fantastic new level.

After a speaking engagement in Georgia I joined a rather large group going to an "order your own pizza creation" restaurant. I was fascinated with the idea of a thin whole wheat crust covered with tomato sauce, adding every vegetable available on top, and then covering it all with salsa before baking.

There were about twenty folks in our group and filled a major portion of the establishment. As the guest of honor, I was given the gift of ordering first. I placed my dream order and the waiter told me he didn't think they had any salsa. I told him we all could go to some other restaurant and try our luck in getting what we wanted there.

Looking at the size our group, he said he would check with the manager and see if he was mistaken about "no salsa." He returned to report that they could get some across the street and that my order would be no problem.

When our pizzas arrived, there was so much interest from other members of our group that I didn't even get a slice of my own creation. The manager was so impressed with the results, he added it to their menu and it was labeled "Howard's Pizza."

I have spent over twenty years pursuing a vegan diet and when I saw what most folks were eating called pizza, I was sure it had been designed by the health care community as an income creator. The work of Dr. McDougall, Dr. Esselstyn, Dr. Campbell and others nailed the fact that what we were eating was the most important factor in our future health.

The overwhelming amount of what was called pizza in America was a direct path to the emergency room. The covering of cheese became larger and then it was added to the crust to the point where they had doubled the amount of cheese in each pizza. In my opinion, cheese is to heart disease what water is to drowning. Vegan pizza was as rare as seeing hair on a frog.

When Mark told me of his idea to write a book about "Heart Healthy Pizza," I became his greatest supporter. I think this book could save more lives than the discovery of penicillin.

"Heart Healthy Pizza" is more than a pizza without cheese. It is about creating one that is added-fat free and nutritious from the pan up, and best of all, tastes great. This book will enable you to obtain all of the health benefits, plus allow you to please the most discerning taste buds to the joy of pizza."

Howard Lyman, author of *The Mad Cowboy* and *No More Bull!*

Introduction

"To eat is a necessity, but to eat intelligently is an art."

--- *Francois de La Rochefoucauld*

"Pizza!" There are few foods that conjure up as much interest, emotional attachment and enjoyment as pizza. In the United States it's the second favorite take-out food behind chicken. An estimated 3 billion pizzas are purchased every year. Not surprisingly, a recent Gallup Poll notes that "children between the ages of 3 and 11 prefer pizza over all other foods for lunch and dinner."

Unfortunately, there is a downside to conventional pizza. The preponderance of cured or cooked meats and various cheeses on the average pizza can be a nutritional nightmare for many reasons, mostly related to the amount of fat (and saturated fat) in both meat and dairy products.

Traditional nutritionists will advise minimizing the amount of meat toppings, using lower fat or smaller amounts of cheeses, and incorporating more vegetables when ordering or making pizzas. Although these recommendations may lessen the potential negative biological impact to one's body, they are by no means true safeguards against many degenerative diseases stemming from dietary abuse, including those of obesity, heart disease, some cancers, and Type II diabetes.

WHAT IS A HEART-HEALTHY PIZZA?

It's not just the meat and/or cheese that is helping to enable heart disease. It is the added oil. Over twenty years of independent peer-reviewed research by Drs. Dean Ornish and Caldwell Esselstyn has demonstrated that a no-added oil plant-based diet can not only reverse heart disease, but in theory, prevent it. Furthermore, studies by Dr. Neal Barnard have indicated that the same diet can reverse Type II diabetes, and the writings of Dr. McDougall point out how added vegetable oils "are easily oxidized, forming free radicals that damage the arteries." A truly heart healthy pizza would not contain any added oil or fat.

Unfortunately, the current generation of non-dairy cheeses, quite remarkable in their gooeyness and melting capabilities, are often as high or higher as their dairy equivalents in unhealthy added fat or oil. Additionally, most are very expensive, and provide little in the way of useful nutrition.

"Is it possible," I wondered, "to develop inexpensive, heart-healthy no-added fat, non-dairy "cheese-like sauces" for a plant-based pizza?

The book in your hands is my answer. For over 5 years now I've been experimenting and testing recipes using a wide variety of grains, legumes, vegetables, assorted liquids, spices, herbs, and thickeners to construct a range of delicate or often firm custard-like "cheese-like" sauces for pizzas. The goal is not to duplicate cheese, but to provide a stimulating and delectable inexpensive alternative.

These recipes are all heart healthy and provide significant nutritional diversity. For the most part they require little effort to make and can easily be adjusted to meet personal preferences. None contain any oil, with salt being optional and not necessary for producing an excellent taste and texture profile.

USING THIS BOOK

This cookbook is for the average cook who wants to be able to make healthy, nutritious, cost-effective, and tasty pizza at home. Full of tips, techniques, and recipes, you'll be able to quickly start creating your own inexpensive homemade pizza and enjoy it even more, knowing that it will be nutritious for both you and those you love.

Here's how this book is organized:

Chapter 1: covers the basics of making a good "pizza foundation," with recipes for different types of crusts, including many for readers on a gluten-free diet.

Chapter 2: provides a variety of bottom sauces to mix'n'match with selected fillings.

Chapter 3: shows how to make many different types of heart healthy cheese-like sauces. They can also be used with pasta, over grains, in stir-fries, quesadillas, as dips, salad dressings, and more.

Chapter 4: makes available recipes and ideas for complete "pizza concepts."

People using this book will have varying levels of experience in making pizza. Those readers who are already adept at making pizza dough or planning to use pre-made crusts or dough, might want to go directly to Chapter 3 and start making non-cheese sauces. Others may want to first take advantage of some of the dough and bottom sauce recipes provided.

There's also a "Resources" section (with online and offline information) covering many topics, and some Appendices that go into greater detail about various nutritional, diet, and health issues mentioned in this book. A "Glossary" is also provided to help learn more about some of the products or ingredients mentioned in these recipes.

Finally, online at the "Heart Healthy Pizza" website and blog, you'll find all the links found in this book, periodic posting of recipes, ideas, and new resources (including access to a large subset of photos taken during the development of these recipes).

My best wishes and blessings to you! I truly hope your experiences in making the "most nutritious pizza in the world" are enjoyable, creative, satisfying, and pleasing... and that as you treat your body to great and truly healthy pizza, your heart and circulatory system will treat you very well in return.

Mark

msutton@hearthealthypizza.com
http://www.hearthealthypizza.com
http://www.youtube.com/user/HeartHealthyPizza

Chapter 1: Firm Foundations

"You better cut the pizza in four pieces because I'm not hungry enough to eat six."

--- Yogi Berra

In this chapter we'll be discussing the ways and means of making a firm foundation for your pizza experiences. A whole book could be written solely on the different methodologies, techniques, and recipes for making pizza-style crusts. As with pizza fillings or toppings it's all somewhat subjective, so Heart Healthy Pizza cooks are urged to go with what they find works and enjoy the results of a little experimentation. Here's some of what I've learned:

THE PROCESS

MAKING THE DOUGH:

Bread machines are fantastic. In less than 10 minutes one can quickly prep all the ingredients for making a pizza dough for the machine, turn it on (using the dough or pizza setting), and have a dough ready in anywhere from 30 minutes to an hour and a half. Once it's confirmed that the dough is working well (proper elasticity before the 1st rise), time can be spent prepping ingredients for the pizza before the dough is ready to shape. Note that it's not necessary to wait for the recommended 2nd rise to be completed if in a hurry, although the 2nd rise does make a better crust.

When using a bread machine, the conventional method is to put the measured warm water in first, then sweetener of choice, the flour(s), which optionally can have some salt mixed in, optional spices or herbs, followed by the yeast. Check the dough a few times before the first rise. It should be elastic and smooth, and "spongy" to the touch, the soft dough having about the texture of an earlobe. Depending upon how accurate the measurements, the dough kneading process might do with a little more water or flour. When adding additional water or flour, use about a tablespoon at a time, wait a few minutes, then assess the results.

When making the dough by hand, the general process is to mix the yeast, sugar, and warm water in a large bowl, waiting 10 to 12 minutes as the mixture starts to bubble and "rise." Then, one adds the flour incrementally and mixes, pouring it out onto a counter (dusted with flour if desired), and kneading the dough, folding it over repeatedly and pressing firmly with the palms of your hands outward until it's elastic and smooth. This will take from 5 to 10 minutes. Put the dough in a bowl (it doesn't necessarily have to be oiled as most books recommend), cover, and let it rise for at least an hour. If the kitchen is drafty or cool, let the dough (still in a glass bowl) rise in an oven set to "Warm." When dough has near doubled in size, "punch" it down with a fist and start the shaping process.

Note: there's also an abundance of pre-made pizza shells available in many stores or establishments, as well as pre-made doughs (be careful! some are high in added oil, always read the nutritional label). Trader Joe's makes three excellent and inexpensive 1 lb. doughs suitable for a medium thin 12" pizza or 14" pizza: whole wheat, white, and white with chopped herbs of choice. Consider, too, checking with a local pizzeria. Often they will sell pre-made dough to you directly!

SHAPING THE DOUGH:

I like to mold or knead the dough by hand initially in the air, letting gravity do some of the stretching work as it's rotated several times, then press the dough onto the cooking surface with hands and fingers working and pressing the dough carefully from inside to near the outside of the perimeter of the pie. Some people like to get a very thin crust by using a rolling pin. The key trick with a rolling pin is to roll in one direction forward, physically turning the pizza between rolls.

Pizzas can be of many different geometrical forms: rectangles, oblong ovals, rounded triangles, smaller circles, and even irregular "amoebas." A particular shape doesn't keep a pizza from being a pizza. As such, have fun and don't worry too much about "symmetrical precision" when making your pizza foundation. Even so, be sure to pay attention to the thickness of the dough or pre-made dough or shell being used in regards to the water content of planned toppings. This will facilitate more reliable results in the pizza-making process and not having a soggy pie.

PIZZA COOKING SURFACE:

My favorite pan to use as of this writing is a fine non-stick baking sheet. For a non-standard non-flour based pizza foundation, a lightly oiled rectangular glass pyrex casserole dish works well. A "spring roll pan" with detachable bottom is great for making a killer deep dish pizza. Some people love their perforated circular pizza pan. Once again, experiment and find out what works best for you.

Pizza stones have recently become popular and more main stream. A pizza stone needs to be pre-heated to be effective. When using a pizza stone, one should put corn meal on a pizza spatula, then the shaped dough on top of it. Now add fillings and sauces. The pizza is then carefully "slid" onto the pizza stone in the oven.

OVEN TEMPERATURE:

In general, most pizzas are cooked at temperatures ranging from 425 to 450 degrees F., the former taking around 15 - 20 minutes, the latter 7 to 8 minutes. The time and temperature used are also impacted by the thickness of your pizza, what type of crust (homemade or pre-made), the size of vegetable toppings and whether they are pre-cooked (or roasted) beforehand. Cutting vegetables a bit smaller than normal will help take advantage of the lesser cooking time required when using a pre-made crust.

Not all ovens are calibrated properly to exact temperature settings or cook evenly inside. You may have to play with the temperature and learn where best to put the pizza a few times to determine what works best with your oven. In general, cooking the pizza in the middle of the oven works well.

TIPS & TECHNIQUES:

- Store flours in the refrigerator or freezer. When making pizza dough, mix the flour(s) in a large bowl, letting it come to room temperature. If kitchen is cold, set your oven for "warm," and put the flour(s) in a Pyrex bowl. Warm the mixture just enough to take the chill off (which slows down the yeast), before using.

- If you're making dough from scratch consider making extra that can be used later. Pizza dough will keep for several days in the refrigerator, and can be used in around two hours (kneed it, put in bowl or on a plate, let come to room temperature). Dough from the refrigerator tends to make a less fluffy and thinner crust, a New York-style pizza in effect. Freezing dough also works well, although the thawing out process will take significantly longer. Frozen dough can usually be stored for about 3 months.

- When making your own dough from scratch, understand that it's akin to making bread. It may take a few tries to recognize and understand the proper elasticity in texture you need to get a good crust. Sometimes you might need to add a little extra water or flour. Once you understand what it feels like, the texture and elasticity that works, it's easy to adjust "on-the-fly."

- You can make your on "pre-made" pizza crusts by covering and freezing the shaped dough for later. To use: assemble with sauces and toppings, cook in a pre-heated 375 degree F. oven until cooked through.

- Some chefs recommend cooking the pizza crust first for several minutes, then cooking with toppings. I've not done this too often. It really depends upon the type of crust. A polenta-style crust can sometimes benefit from having a little pre-baking. The same holds true for many gluten-free pizza crusts.

- 1 packet of yeast is equal to 2 1/4 teaspoons. Store yeast in refrigerator or freezer (especially if in a jar). Let measured amount come to room temperature before using.

- Some people recommend "proofing" the yeast before using when making dough by hand. This involves mixing a small amount of the total yeast to be used into a small amount of warm water in a small bowl until it dissolves, then putting the bowl in a warm place, and waiting around 10 to 12 minutes. If a layer of foam doesn't arise, it's best to get fresher yeast.

- Often, less water is needed for a recipe that is kneaded by hand than the same recipe made with a bread machine.

PIZZA FOUNDATION RECIPES

There are quite a few different pizza crust recipes available on the Internet and in books, depending upon ingredients and size of pizza desired. Below are some basic and unique recipes for pizza foundations:

Basic Pizza Dough

INGREDIENTS:
- 3/4 cup warm water
- 1 t. sugar (or sweetener of choice)
- 1 T. oil (optional)
- 1/2 t. salt (optional)
- 2 1/4 cups all-purpose or bread flour
- 2 to 2 1/4 t. yeast (1 packet)

METHOD (Bread Machine):

1. Put in warm water 1st, optional oil, sweetener, flours (pre-stirred with

optional salt), and yeast.

2. Select "Pizza" or "Dough" setting on the bread machine and press "Start."

VARIATIONS:

- Substitute 1 cup of the flour above with 1 cup of cornmeal, soy flour, or semolina flour. The addition of semolina flour makes for a slightly nuttier taste and lighter texture.

NOTES:

- The dough can be used after the first rise, although 2nd rise is preferred.
- Granulated sugar, agave nectar, molasses, rice syrup, barley syrup, or maple syrup can also be used as sweeteners.
- This is for 2 thin 12" crusts, 1 large thin (if rectangular, 10" x 24"), or 1 thicker 12" crust. About 2 lbs. of dough and 8 servings.

Whole Wheat Dough

INGREDIENTS:

- 1 cup of warm water
- 1 T. oil (optional)
- 1 T. sugar (or sweetener of choice)
- 1 t. salt (optional)
- 1 cup whole wheat flour
- 1 1/2 cup bread flour
- 2 1/4 t. yeast (1 packet)

NOTE:

- This is for 2 thin 12" crusts, 1 large thin (if rectangular, 10" x 24"), or 1 thicker 12" crust. About 2 lbs. of dough and 8 servings.

Pumpernickel or Rye Dough

INGREDIENTS:

- 1 1/3 to 1 2/3 cups warm water
- 1 T. oil (optional)
- 2 T. molasses

- 1 1/2 cup bread flour
- 3/4 cup rye flour
- 2 T. cocoa powder
- 2 t. coffee granules (optional)
- 1 T. caraway seeds
- 1 t. salt (optional)
- 1 1/2 t. yeast

NOTES:

- To make "rye crust" instead, omit cocoa flour & coffee granules.
- This is for 2 thin 12" crusts, 1 large thin (if rectangular, 10" x 24"), or 1 thicker 12" crust. About 2 lbs. of dough and 8 servings.

Wheat and Millet Dough

INGREDIENTS:

- 1 cup warm water
- 1 T. sugar (or sweetener of choice)
- 1 1/2 cup whole wheat flour
- 1 1/2 cup millet flour
- 1/2 t. salt
- 2 1/4 t. yeast

METHOD:

1. Add water and sugar to bread machine, stir until the sugar is dissolved.
2. Mix flours and salt in a separate bowl.
3. Add flour mixture to bread machine, then yeast.
4. Turn on bread machine with the setting of "Pizza" or "Dough."

NOTE:

- Depending upon accuracy of flour measurements, an additional 2 to 3 T. of water might be needed during the first kneading cycle to get proper elasticity.

Wheat and Black Bean Dough

INGREDIENTS:

- 3/4 cups black beans (about 1/2 a 15 oz. can)
- 1/3 cup water
- 2/3 cups warm water
- 1 1/4 t. sugar (or sweetener of choice)
- 2 1/4 t. yeast
- 1 1/2 cup bread flour
- 1 cup wheat flour
- 1/2 t. salt (optional)

METHOD:

1. Rinse and drain beans, then puree in a blender or food processor with 1/3 cup water until smooth. Add water as necessary (in 1 T. increments).
2. Whisk together warm water, sugar, yeast, and bean puree.
3. Mix together flours and salt, add slowly to yeast mixture (if not using a bread machine, stir as flour mixture is added).
4. Knead until the dough is elastic, let rise, covered, for at least an hour.
5. Pre-heat oven to 425 degrees F.
6. Shape pizza dough on a lightly oiled non-stick baking sheet.
7. Arrange toppings and sauce(s) on top of shaped dough.
8. Bake 15 to 20 minutes (or until toppings are cooked through).

NOTES:

- Whether making dough by hand or with a bread machine, it might be necessary to adjust the amount of flour or water in 1 T. increments to get proper elasticity.
- This recipes makes two finely textured 12 to 14" pizza crusts.

GLUTEN-FREE:

Corn Polenta

INGREDIENTS:

- 1 cup cornmeal (roasted corn meal, if available)

- 2 cups water
- 1/4 t. salt (optional)
- 1 cup low fat soy milk (or water)
- ground black pepper (to taste)

METHOD:

1. Bring water or milk and salt to a slow boil in a pot. Whisk in cornmeal at first, and then stir repeatedly with wooden spoon carefully at a simmer to reduce lumps. Sprinkle in pepper. Stirring frequently, the polenta should thicken sufficiently in 10 to 20 minutes (the spoon will stand up straight in the polenta and not fall down). Remove from heat, let rest a few minutes.
2. Spread the cooked polenta onto a non-stick baking sheet in a lightly oiled 9 x 13" glass baking dish. Use a little water on fingertips or the back of a spoon/spatula, if necessary, to smooth the surface and help with shaping.
3. Bake polenta at 400 degrees F. until firm and the bottom and edges start to get crisp and golden (about 20 to 30 minutes).
4. Add toppings and sauce(s), and put back into oven for 20 to 30 minutes (until toppings are cooked). If desired, lightly broil for a few minutes.

NOTE:

1. A lightly oiled casserole dish works well, and will generally make for a thicker crust. A knife and fork might be needed to eat this entree.

Millet Polenta

INGREDIENTS:

- 1 cup millet
- 3 to 3 1/4 cups water
- 1/4 t. salt (optional)

METHOD:

1. Bring millet, water, and salt to a slow boil. Cover, simmer for 40 to 45 minutes, stirring occasionally. The polenta should be very thick.
2. Uncover, let come to room temperature. Hard stir mixture with a wooden or plastic spoon to make it thick.
3. Pre-heat oven to 375 degrees F.

4. Lightly oil a 9" x 13" glass baking dish. Spoon millet mixture into baking dish, and flatten/press/smooth it down with the back of a large spoon or your hand (dampen if necessary).
5. Cool polenta in the refrigerator for at least an hour (it will firm up).
6. Add toppings and sauces of choice.
7. Bake for 30 minutes (or until vegetables and sauce are cooked through).

VARIATIONS:
- Mix in dried red pepper flakes or ground cumin to taste to millet polenta before shaping in baking dish.

Whole Grain Rice and Chickpea Flour

INGREDIENTS:
- 1 cup uncooked brown rice
- 1 cup zucchini or yellow squash (shredded)
- 2 T. flax seeds
- 1/2 cup water
- 1/3 cup chickpea flour
- 1/2 T. dried Italian herbs

METHOD:
1. Add rice to 2 cups water in small pot. Bring to a boil, and simmer, covered, around 40 minutes (until the liquid is absorbed).
2. Stir rice a few times, and let sit, covered, until coming to room temperature.
3. Pre-heat oven to 425 degrees F.
4. Lightly grease a 9" x 13" glass baking dish.
5. Grind flax seeds in a spice mill and whisk into water.
6. Add cooked rice, chickpea flour, herbs, and water/flax mixture to a large mixing bowl. Mix and combine ingredients using a large wooden or plastic spoon (using your hands and fingers, adding more water if necessary).
7. Press mixture down into the baking dish to create a rectangular, firm, and smooth dough crust. Dampen fingers if need be to smooth the mixture on top. This recipe makes a thick foundation.
8. Bake, uncovered, for about 10 minutes (the bottom will begin to crust).

9. Remove from oven, add toppings, sauce(s) of choice.

10. Bake an additional 15 to 20 minutes, or until the toppings are cooked to taste.

11. Let cool before serving. Cut slices using a knife and spatula.

Buckwheat and Chickpea Flour Crust

INGREDIENTS:

- 3/4 cup of warm water
- 2 1/4 t. yeast
- 1 1/2 t. sugar (or sweetener of choice)
- 1 T. flax seeds
- 1 1/2 cup buckwheat flour
- 1/2 cup chickpea flour
- 1/2 t. salt (optional)
- 1 1/2 t. dried herbs of choice

METHOD:

1. Whisk water, yeast, and sugar in a large mixing bowl.

2. Grind flax seeds in a spice mill. Mix into yeast mixture. Cover, let rise for 10 to 12 minutes.

3. Mix remaining ingredients together in a separate bowl, and slowly add to yeast mixture, stirring with a large spoon. Strive for a thick dough that's not too sticky, adding water or buckwheat flour in 1 tablespoons increments if necessary.

4. Cover and let rise 45 minutes to 1 hour.

5. Pre-heat oven to 425 degrees F.

6. Form into a large dough ball and press into a lightly oiled non-stick baking pan. Press dough into desired shape with fingers, moving out from the center. Lightly wet fingers if necessary to aid in the shaping process.

7. Bake in oven for 5 to 7 minutes.

8. Arrange toppings and sauce(s) on dough, bake for 10 to 15 minutes (or until toppings are cooked).

NOTE:

- This recipe makes a thick 12 to 14" pizza.

Oat Flour Crust

INGREDIENTS:

- 2 1/2 cups rolled oats
- 1 cup warm water
- 2 1/4 t. yeast
- 1 t. sugar (or sweetener of choice)
- 1 to 2 T. flax seeds
- 2 t. dried Italian herbs
- 1/2 t. salt (optional)

METHOD:

1. Whisk together water, yeast, and sugar in a large mixing bowl. Cover, let rise for 10 to 12 minutes.
2. Grind flax seeds in a spice mill and mix into yeast mixture.
3. Put oats into a blender or food processor to make oat flour (about 2 cups worth).
4. Mix remaining ingredients together and slowing add to the yeast mixture, stirring with a large spoon. Gradually fold dough into a large flat ball (the dough will be stiff).
5. Cover and let rise for 30 to 45 minutes.
6. Pre-heat oven to 425 degrees F.
7. Shape into a ball with your hands, and press the dough into a lightly oiled non-stick baking pan into the shape desired. If necessary, lightly wet your fingers to help with the shaping process.
8. Bake in oven for 5 minutes (crust's bottom should be starting to turn brown).
9. Arrange toppings and sauce(s) on dough, bake for 10 to 15 minutes (or until toppings are cooked).

NOTE:

- This recipe makes a 12 to 14" pizza.

Rice and Potato Crust

INGREDIENTS:

- 1 1/4 cup rice flour (white or brown)
- 1/2 cup potato starch
- 1 T. flax seeds
- 1 cup warm water
- 2 t. yeast
- 1 t. sugar
- 1 to 1 1/2 t. of dried herbs of choice
- 1/2 t. salt (optional)

METHOD:

1. Whisk together water, yeast, and sugar in a large mixing bowl. Cover, and let rise for 12 minutes.
2. Grind flax seeds in a spice mill, add to yeast mixture (stirring a few times).
3. Mix flour, starch, and herbs together in a separate bowl. Slowing add this to the yeast mixture, stirring with a large spoon. Cover, and let rise for 30 to 45 minutes.
4. Pre-heat oven to 425 degrees.
5. Shape dough into a ball with your hands. If too wet, add a little more rice flour in 1 T. increments. Press dough ball into a lightly oiled non-stick baking pan to shape desired. If necessary, lightly wet fingers.
6. Bake for 5 minutes (dough should be getting firm).
7. Arrange toppings and sauce(s) on dough, bake for 10 to 15 minutes (or until toppings are cooked).

NOTE:

- This recipe makes a 12 to 14" pizza.

Chapter 2: Amazing Gracious Sauces

"SAUCE, n. The one infallible sign of civilization and enlightenment. A people with no sauces has one thousand vices; a people with one sauce has only nine hundred and ninety-nine. For every sauce invented and accepted a vice is renounced and forgiven."

--- Ambrose Bierce

Whether it's tomato-based or not, just about everyone enjoys a good sauce on their pizza. Even so, it's worth noting that some people prefer their sauce on the actual pizza's crust, while others prefer cheese directly on the crust followed by fillings, then a tasty sauce. With this in mind, the recipes in this chapter are mostly thought of as being for the bottom of a pizza, but they are certainly not limited to that position in any pizza ecosystem. They've been divided loosely into three categories: red, green, and "white" for convenience.

TIPS & TECHNIQUES:

- 1 cup of sauce is generally used for a 12" to 14" pizza, although opinions do vary. Too much sauce (especially if not very thick) might not only be quite messy when eating, but may cause everything on top of the crust to slide off inappropriately. Any pizza leftover the next day might also be unduly soggy.

- Pressed for time? Try spreading tomato paste on top of the pizza foundation, sprinkle it with red chili flakes (or herbs and/or spices of choice), add the filling vegetables and then a topping sauce.

- If using a thick cream-like sauce on top of the crust, gently press the filling vegetables into the sauce.

- Sprinkling herbs and/or spices on top of the foundation before adding vegetables or a sauce can work very well.

- Finely diced mushrooms provide an interesting texture and taste on top of a sauce before other vegetables are layered and positioned. They may add more moisture, so make sure the crust used isn't too thin.

- Sometimes the best "bottom" sauce is the most simple. Grab a jar of salsa and spread it on the foundation.

- Use canned, drained, and slightly chopped or "squished" tomatoes for a quick non-sauce approach. If good quality tomatoes are readily available, try using herbed or seasoned slices of raw tomatoes instead of a tomato sauce. The rich flavor really "explodes" when munched in the completed pie.

- Be creative! Use left-over chili, stew, or a thickened marinade for a bottom sauce.

- If the sauce is on the thin side, using more watery vegetables on top of it (such as summer squashes) might make thin crust pieces "floppy" from the extra moisture.

- Left-over sauce can be a nice addition to a soups, steamed vegetables, or pasta, as a spread, or in a wrap with lettuce, vegetables, and beans. Slighting thinning out some leftover sauces with liquid will make them suitable for use as a salad dressings.

- Most brands of commercially available canned tomatoes have low or no salt versions (the American Heart Association recommends no more than around 3/4 teaspoon of salt per day in one's diet: 1500 mg.). Always read the label before purchasing.

RED SAUCE RECIPES:

Classic Tomato Sauce

INGREDIENTS:
- 2 to 3 cloves of garlic chopped
- 1 small onion chopped (around 1/2 cup)
- 2 medium tomatoes finely diced (or 1 14.5 oz can chopped tomatoes)
- 1/2 cup water (plus 1/4 cup red wine or water)
- 1/2 T. low-sodium Tamari (or soy sauce)
- 1/2 cup diced fresh basil (1 T. dried basil)
- 1 T. red wine vinegar or balsamic vinegar
- 4 oz. (1/2 can) tomato paste (or as desired)
- pinch of salt (optional)
- ground pepper (to taste)

METHOD:
1. Steam fry garlic and onions in a little of the initial liquid until soft (add more liquid if needed). This is done by bringing the liquid to a medium simmer and frequently "stirring" the vegetables until they are tender.
2. Stir in tomatoes, Tamari, vinegar and simmer on very low until flavors blend (10 to 15 minutes).
3. Mix in tomato paste, salt, and pepper, let simmer another 5 minutes.

4. Turn off heat, cover, and let come to room temperature.

VARIATIONS:
- If using canned tomatoes, drain, reserve liquid to use in place of water.
- Add a little Tabasco sauce or chopped green peppers to vegetables for steam-frying.
- Substitute or add other herbs: rosemary, marjoram, oregano.
- Adding drained capers and a little "spicy heat" (red chili pepper flakes, chopped hot peppers) and using fresh or dried parsley instead of basil makes a puttanesca sauce.

NOTE:
- This recipe makes approximately 2 cups of sauce.

Raw Tomato Sauce

INGREDIENTS:
- 2 medium tomatoes coarsely chopped (optionally peeled, about 2 cups)
- 1/4 cup raisins
- 1 T. lemon juice
- 2 cloves garlic (peeled and minced)
- 1 T. nutritional yeast (optional)
- 1/2 to 1 t. dried Italian herb(s) of choice
- ground black pepper (to taste)
- 1/8 to 1/4 cup water

METHOD:
1. Cover raisins with water and let soak until plump (45 min. to 1 hour).
1. Chop up the tomatoes, add to blender.
2. Add remaining ingredients and pulse a few times. Blend to desired consistency and let sit 5 to 10 minutes.

VARIATION:
- Mix in some dried or fresh chopped herbs (to taste) after blending.

NOTES:

- The amount of water used will vary with the juiciness of the tomatoes. Strive for a "thick pureed gazpacho" texture.
- Makes around 2 cups of sauce.

Quick Italian Tomato Sauce

INGREDIENTS:

- 1/2 t. onion powder
- 1/2 t. garlic powder
- 1-2 T dried herbs/spices of choice
- 1 8 oz. can tomato paste
- 8 oz. of liquid (use the tomato paste can as a measure, add more if desired)
- 1/2 t. salt (optional
- 1 T. nutritional yeast (optional)

METHOD:

1. Whisk together all ingredients (or blend vigorously using a spoon).
2. Can be put on pizza directly or (preferred) put into a sauce pan and simmered on low to medium heat until the flavors blend (about 5 to 10 minutes).

Red Tomato Salsa

INGREDIENTS:

- 2 cloves garlic
- 1/2 medium onion
- 1 to 2 jalapeno peppers (de-seeding is optional)
- 1/2 green pepper
- 1/4 to 1/3 cup chopped fresh basil, parsley, or cilantro
- 2 medium tomatoes
- 2 T. red wine or apple vinegar
- 1 T. ground cumin
- pinch of salt (optional)

METHOD:

1. Coarsely chop all vegetables by hand.
2. In a food processor, using the "S" blade, pulse chop the garlic, onions, peppers, and basil or cilantro. Don't blend too much to where you have liquified the mixture.
3. Add the tomatoes and pulse chop a few times, with caution.
4. Empty into a large glass bowl, mix in the rest of the ingredients. The salsa will taste best if allowed to sit for at least an hour or more, stirred occasionally.

VARIATIONS:

- Toast cumin seeds in the oven then grind in spice blender. Mix in after all processing is done.
- Roast chopped vegetables under a broiler before pulsing.
- Roast 1/2 to 1 cup cooked corn kernels and mix in after processing is done.

NOTE:

- Makes 2 1/2 to 3 cups of salsa.

Carrot Sauce

INGREDIENTS:

- 2 cups of carrots (peeling optional, sliced crosswise in 1/4" slices))
- 1 cup of water
- 1 clove garlic (mined)
- 1/4 cup onion (diced)
- 1/2 t. dried basil
- 1 T. blond miso
- 1 T. flax seeds (optional)

METHOD:

1. Grind flax seeds in a spice mill.
2. Bring vegetables, basil, and enough water to cover them to a boil (stirring), simmer on low, covered, around 15 minutes until fork tender.
3. Let cool to room temperature. Drain (reserving any leftover liquid).
4. Pulse chop vegetables with miso and flax seeds, gradually adding 1 to 1

1/2 cups leftover liquid (or water) until obtaining desired thickness.

VARIATIONS:

- Substitute 1 cup of peeled cubed & cooked sweet potatoes or 1 medium beet for 1 cup of carrots.
- Use 1/2 t. ground ginger instead of basil.
- Use 1 t. curry powder in place of basil.
- Mix in some dried or fresh chopped parsley after making sauce.

NOTE:

- Makes approximately 2 1/2 cups of sauce.

Tangy Blenderized BBQ Sauce

INGREDIENTS:

- 8 oz. pineapple chunks in own juice (undrained)
- 1 can (8 oz.) tomato paste
- 1/3 cup diced onion
- 1 t. garlic powder
- 1/2 t. dry mustard
- 1/2 t. red chili pepper flakes
- 1/2 t. ground cumin
- 1/2 t. ground paprika
- 1/2 t. ground ginger
- 1 T. soy sauce
- 1 t. liquid smoke
- 2 T. vinegar of choice
- 1 1/4 cup liquid
- 1 T. Ener-G
- 1/4 t. ground black pepper (to taste)

METHOD:

1. Add all ingredients into a blender or food processor and blend until it's a smooth sauce.
2. Put sauce into a pot and simmer 5-10 minutes until it thickens, stirring frequently.

Thousand Island Dressing Sauce

INGREDIENTS:

- 1 box Mori Lite Extra Firm Tofu (12.3 oz.)
- 1 T. prepared horseradish
- 1/4 t. dry mustard
- 2 T. red wine vinegar
- 3 T. tomato paste
- 4 T. water
- 1/2 t. salt
- 1/2 cup chopped sweet pickles

METHOD:

1. Blend all ingredients except for pickles. Add additional water, 1 T. at a time, if the mixture is too thick until it's a smoother sauce.
2. Fold pickles in after blending.

GREEN SAUCE RECIPES:

Basil Pesto

INGREDIENTS:

- 1 cup chopped fresh basil (de-stemmed)
- 1/4 cup sunflower seeds (soaked for a day or overnight, drained)
- 2 T. lemon juice
- 1/2 cup tofu (firm or extra-firm)
- 1/2 cup water
- 2 t. garlic powder (or 2 cloves garlic, peeled and chopped)
- 1 T. nutritional yeast
- 1 T. blond miso (optional, or to taste)

METHOD:

1. Add all ingredients to a food processor, reserving the water. Pulse the mixture a few times, then gradually increase the speed of the processing as water is slowly added until the pesto has a smooth consistency.

VARIATIONS:

- Spinach and raw walnut pieces
- Parsley and raw sunflower seeds
- Cilantro and toasted pumpkin seeds

Rosemary Pesto

INGREDIENTS:

- 1/3 cup chopped fresh rosemary (de-stemmed)
- 1/3 cup sunflower seeds (soaked for a day, drained, or overnight)
- 2 T. lemon juice
- 1/2 cup tofu (firm or extra-firm)
- 2 t. garlic powder
- 1 T. Ener-G
- 3/4 cup water

METHOD:

1. Add all ingredients to a food processor, reserving the water. Pulse the mixture a few times, then gradually increase the speed of the processing as water is slowly added until the pesto has a smooth consistency.

Green Tomato Salsa

INGREDIENTS:

- 2 cloves garlic
- 1 small jalapeno (seeded, more to taste)
- 1/2 medium white/yellow onion
- 6 tomatillos or 2 medium green tomatoes
- 1/4 cup chopped cilantro
- 1 T. lime juice
- 1/2 T. apple cider vinegar
- 1 T. ground cumin
- pinch of salt (optional)

METHOD:

1. Coarsely chop all vegetables
2. Add garlic, jalapeno(s), onion, and cilantro
3. Pulse chop (on/off frequently) to get chunky consistency but not to blend.
4. Add tomatillos or tomatoes, pulse chop carefully.
5. Empty into large glass bowl, stir in remaining ingredients. Tastes best if allow to sit for at least an hour or more, stirring occasionally.

VARIATION:

• Roast all vegetables before pulsing.

NOTE:

• This recipe makes around 2 1/2 cups of salsa.

Mucho Mocko Guaco

INGREDIENTS:

• 2 cups of frozen peas (approximately 10 oz.)
• 1/2 cup tofu (preferably lite)
• 3 garlic cloves minced
• 1/4 cup onion (finely diced)
• 1 tomato (diced)
• 1/2 T. ground cumin
• 1/2 t. dried oregano
• 1 T. lemon or lime juice
• pinch of salt
• 1/2 t. Tabasco sauce (to taste)

METHOD:

1. Cook peas according to package instructions.
2. Blend drained & cooled peas with tofu, garlic, and lemon or lime juice in a food processor until smooth. Scrape from the side of the food processor if necessary. If too thick, add water in 1 T. increments until sauce is smooth.
3. Mix blended tofu and peas with remaining ingredients in a large bowl.

VARIATIONS:

- Add sliced jalapenos (to taste) to the blended tofu and remaining ingredients.
- 2 cups of peeled, chopped, and steamed peeled broccoli stems can be used in place of the peas.
- Add additional lemon or lime juice to taste.
- Add chopped cilantro or parsley.

NOTE:

• Makes around 2 1/2 to 3 cups.

"WHITE" SAUCE RECIPES:

Lite Light Brown-White Sauce

INGREDIENTS:

- 1 1/2 cups of non-dairy milk (see Note below)
- 3 T. flour
- 1 T. nutritional yeast
- 1/2 t. onion powder
- 1/2 t. dry mustard
- 1 T. white wine (see Note below))
- 1 T. blond miso (optional)
- ground pepper to taste

METHOD:

1. Blend all ingredients in blender.
2. Pour into sauce pan on medium heat until it starts to boil, drop temperature to low, stirring frequently, until thickened as desired. Remove from heat and let cool to room temperature.

VARIATIONS:

- Add 1/2 to 1/3 cooked sliced or diced carrots before blending.

- Add 1/4 cup chopped nuts of choice.
- 1 - 2 t. of dried or fresh herbs or spices of choice (to taste) after blending.
- Substitute white wine with water or lemon juice.
- Use all-purpose flour instead of wheat flour.

NOTES:
- Non-dairy milks: low /no fat soy milk, almond milk, rice milk, and oat milk.
- Makes around 1 1/2 cups of sauce.

Tofu Ricotta

INGREDIENTS:
- 1 lb. extra-firm or firm tofu
- 2 T. lemon or lime juice
- 1/2 t. garlic powder
- 1/2 t. ground black pepper
- 1/2 t. salt (optional, to taste)
- water (if needed)

METHOD:
1. Combine all ingredients in a large bowl, and, using a fork or potato masher, mash until the tofu mixture has a ricotta-like texture. Add a tablespoon or two of water if needed.

VARIATIONS:
- Add nutritional yeast (to taste).
- Add chopped, cooked, and drained spinach.
- Add chopped fresh or dried herbs.
- Add 1/2 to 1 T. of sweetener of choice.

Polynesian Sauce

INGREDIENTS:
- 1 cup pineapple juice
- 1 T. soy sauce
- 2 T. rice, apple, or white vinegar

- 2 T. brown sugar
- 1 T. ketchup or tomato paste
- 1 t. red pepper flakes
- 1 t. garlic powder
- 1/2 t. ground ginger
- 1 1/2 to 2 T. corn starch

METHOD:

1. Whisk together all ingredients, except cornstarch. Put into a sauce pan or pot. Whisk corn starch with 3 T. of sauce, add back to pot. Gradually bring mixture to a boil, stirring occasionally.
2. Quickly lower the heat to a simmer, stirring periodically until the sauce thickens.
3. Turn off heat and let cool to room temperature.

VARIATION:

- Use 1/8 cup Sherry plus 1/8 cup water instead of 1/4 cup water.

NOTE:

- Makes a little over 1 cup of sauce.

Indian Spice White Sauce

INGREDIENTS

- 1 package Mori Lite Tofu (12.3 oz., extra-firm or firm)
- 1/2 t. garlic powder
- 2 T. corn starch
- 1 t. ground ginger
- 1 t. dried parsley
- 1 1/2 T. lemon juice

METHOD:

1. Put all ingredients into a blender or food processor (preferred), and pulse a few times. Use a spatula (or large wooden or plastic spoon) if necessary to manually stir the mixture a few times, and/or scrap down the sides of your processing device. If too thick, add 1 T. water or more as necessary.

Corn Comfort Sauce

INGREDIENTS:

- 1 15.25 oz. can no-salt corn (about 1 1/2 cups)
- 3/4 cup water
- 1 1/2 T. corn starch
- 1/2 t. dried oregano
- 1/4 to 1/2 t. garlic powder
- pinch of salt (optional)
- ground black pepper (to taste)

METHOD:

1. Drain corn.
2. Process all ingredients in a blender or food processor.
3. Heat over low-med heat, stirring frequently for about 10 minutes until the sauce starts to thicken. Let cool to room temperature before using.

VARIATION:

- Add 1/2 t. sugar (or sweetener of choice) while stirring.
- Add 1/2 t. cumin and/or 1/4 t. chili powder during blending.

NOTE:

- Makes just under 2 cups of sauce.

Mark's Mashed-Up Potatoes Sauce

INGREDIENTS:

- 2 medium potatoes (peeled, in 1/2" dice, around 2 cups total)
- 2 cloves garlic (chopped)
- 14 peppercorns (color as desired!)
- 1/4 t. salt (optional)
- 2 T. flax seeds
- 2 t. prepared horseradish
- 1/2 t. paprika
- 3/4 to 1 cup water (or cooking broth)

METHOD:

1. Put potatoes, garlic, peppercorns, and salt into a small pot. Cover with water.
2. Bring slowly to a boil, stirring a few times. Cover pot and let mixture simmer for 15 to 25 minutes.
3. Drain vegetables and reserve liquid. Let both cool to room temperature.
4. Put vegetables in a blender or food processor. Add remaining ingredients except for water or broth.
5. Add liquid 1/4 cup at a time, slowly increasing the speed of processing until desired thickness is reached. More or less water may be needed depending upon the potatoes used.

VARIATIONS:

- Indian: add ground cumin, coriander and/or garam masala to taste.
- Herbal: add dried herbs.
- Cheezy: add 2 T. of nutritional yeast (to taste).

NOTE:

- This makes around 2 cups of sauce.

Oriental Sauce

INGREDIENTS:

- 1 t. minced garlic
- 1 t. minced fresh ginger
- 1/3 cup liquid of choice (water, Sherry, white wine, sake, broth)
- 1 T. low-sodium Tamari (or soy sauce)
- 2 T. hoisin sauce
- 1/4 t. ground black pepper
- 1/2 t. red chili pepper flakes
- 1 T. rice vinegar (or vinegar of choice)
- 1 1/2 T. corn starch
- 2/3 cups water
- 1 T. roasted sesame seeds (roasting optional)

METHOD:

1. Lightly stir-fry garlic and ginger in 1/4 cup liquid for 2 minutes.
2. Turn heat very low, and add next six ingredients, mixing them in with a large spoon.
3. Let cook for 3 minutes.
4. Whisk together corn starch, water, and sesame seeds.
5. Slowly add corn starch mixture while stirring. Turn heat up to medium low.
6. Bring to simmer, and stir frequently until sauce starts to thicken.
7. Turn off heat and let sauce cool to room temperature.

VARIATIONS:

- Depending upon intended use of the sauce, add chopped scallions and/or other vegetables when stir-frying garlic and ginger.
- Substitute chili garlic sauce of hoisin sauce, omitting red chili pepper flakes.
- Add 1 T. orange marmalade or preserves.

NOTE:

- Makes around 1 cup of sauce.

Chapter 3: No Nonsense Non-Cheeses

"Thou shouldst eat to live; not live to eat."

--- Marcus Tullius Cicero

In this chapter you'll learn how to make tasty and pleasing no-added oil plant-based "cheese-like" sauces using various combinations of whole grains, vegetables, and legumes. The goal is not to duplicate cheese, but instead to create a vibrant, enjoyable, and healthy alternative. Texture, taste, and color are all taken into consideration when making these sauces.

The sauces range from velvety to custardy in terms of texture. The tastes of these sauces range from relatively unseasoned (to use on a pizza with toppings that have a lot of "heat" or spice to them), to those that have more complexity (herbal, spicy, sweet, tangy, etc.). The color will generally be on continuums of white, beige, yellow, orange, and red. Some will have a green tint, while others lean towards brown.

As Heart Healthy Pizza cooks gain more experience in making these sauces, they will begin to quickly learn how to manipulate original recipe ingredients to obtain different textures, tastes, and colors. The following is a general break-down of the process of making these sauces followed by some additional advice and considerations.

THE PROCESS

The base ingredients for any topping sauce will generally be comprised of vegetables, legumes, and or whole grains. The addition of small amounts of nutritional yeast, different mustards, or steamed carrots, as examples, affects the color of the topping and gives it a cheesy taste depending upon the method employed.

Different herbs, spices, and specials (such as fresh basil, sage, Tabasco sauce) can then be used. Sometimes we'll add nuts or seeds in the form of cashews , walnuts, pecans, and sunflower seeds, but generally in a minimal fashion due to their high fat content. Next, a binder or thickener might be used, such as flour, corn starch, Ener-G, or ground flax seeds. Experimentation with different kinds of liquids is also great sport. They can add an interesting background taste to the successful sauce.

The overall results? These topping sauce recipes have a variety of tastes and textures, with the texture ranging from delightfully "firm custard-like" to a rich and smooth velvet experience. In general they are inexpensive, high in fiber, very low in fat, and easy to make. The general method is to process the ingredients in a food processor or blender until a thick almost pancake-like batter is achieved, mix in any extras (spices and/or herbs), pour the sauce on (or under) pizza toppings, and engage the oven. The need to broil the top of the pizza towards the end of cooking depends upon the sauce type, and usually isn't necessary.

TIPS & TECHNIQUES:

- Unless you are using a really high-end blender like a Vita-Mix, it's important that you start with the cooked grains, tofu, or cooked legumes in a blender first, then add liquid and/or nuts slowly in small incremental amounts. A blender can easily be blown out by the nuts getting caught between the blades and base connection, frying the motor. It's most advisable to pulse the device used a few times at first when adding nuts with liquid and then add the other ingredients. Increase the speed of processing slowly. A good food processor can be quite useful in making these recipes. The bottom line: when using nuts and a blender, be careful.

- Some cooked grains are grainier than others. For example, with millet or barley, a longer blending time is needed to get the sauce very smooth eliminating any graininess. The same holds true when using artichokes due to the high fiber content. This is not as much an issue with rice. When using oats, slowly blend your sauce at first, gradually increasing processing speed. Scraping a thick partially-processed sauce down the sides of a blender or food processor with a spatula or spoon is sometimes helpful in obtaining a better blending process.

- The types of nuts are generally interchangeable, the main difference being the amount of fat in the nut of choice. Hence, cashews will provide a greater taste feel than almonds. Almonds will make a lighter and more delicate sauce. Use only raw, unsalted, unroasted nuts.

- Nutritional yeast or wet mustard will add a type of cheesy taste, with the mustard more towards that of a lightly processed dairy cheese. Experiment with different wet mustards such as Brown'n'Spicy, Dijon, Classic plain, or Stone Ground.

- The addition of some steamed carrots, tumeric or paprika, as examples, will shift the sauces' color towards a light orange color, which is sometimes desirable. Carrots add an element of sweetness which may need to be compensated for by adding a little "heat" or spice.

- Sprinkling chili powder, paprika, and other dried herbs on the topping sauce after it's been poured over toppings adds a nice taste as well as visual effect.

- A 425 to 450 degrees F. oven will thicken the sauce without pre-cooking, so none of these recipes require pre-cooking. Most will benefit from being allowed to sit a few minutes after being put on a pizza and to thicken a bit more before baking.

- For an effective time-saving approach, when you're cooking grains for another meal, cook extra and save the leftovers in the refrigerator. They can later be used to make a quick topping sauce. Let the leftover grains come to room temperature while making the dough and vegetable toppings while saving energy too!

- While the dough is being made in the bread machine, pre-layer the sauce ingredients (except for liquid) in your food processor, to then blend after the dough is shaped and the toppings laid out. If using a blender, you should add the nuts in small amounts, pulsing several times before getting to a full smooth blend.

- When pouring your "cheese-like" sauce on your pizza, try experimenting with spirals, a lattice, rows, and even clumps of topping sauce (similar to pieces of whole mozzarella on a conventional pizza).

- Some of the thicker sauces benefit from using the back of a spoon or a spatula to carefully spread on pizza filling ingredients without moving them around. The sauces can usually be poured on from the blender or food processor, although some Heart Healthy cooks might prefer using a large spoon or ladle.

- Spices won't seriously affect the viscosity of the sauce, so feel free to experiment! Keep in mind that adding them to the blending process might result in some unusual colors. Sometimes adding chopped herbs (dry or fresh) to a sauce after it's been blended makes for a great taste.

- Stop and taste the topping sauce being made during the blending process. Take careful note of how thick it is and if the seasoning isn't to your own preference. Sometimes, whether from measurements, amount of water in ingredients, and so forth, there may be a need make some adjustments. Adding the water incrementally, and gauging the viscosity of the sauce, is the best way to avoid a sauce that's too thin. Some people have found that when using a Vitamix, they can so effectively blend the ingredients that they often need less water.

- Leftover topping sauces can be used quite effectively with pasta, on vegetables, in soups, on sandwiches, in quesadillas, as modified salad dressings, and as spreads or dips.

- Try experimenting with using other liquids rather than water. As examples: sake with water, vermouth (in small amounts), wine, beer, left-over broth, and sherry.

- Cooked beans (especially if canned) often provide a wonderful "parmesanish" texture to a topping sauce, let alone excellent nutrition.

- When learning how to master these sauces, it's useful to write down the amount of ingredients used and the results for later reference or recipe tweaking. The Heart Healthy cook may want to increase or decrease suggested amounts of thickeners or liquids, in particular, to suit the taste and texture preferred. My own preferences lean towards a slightly blander sauce than most preferring to add my "heat and/or herbs" to the filling or sprinkling on top of the sauce to taste.

You can also use these recipes by pre-cooking on the stove, Thin leftover sauce swith a little liquid. They will thicken, and can be used on veggies, in stir-fries, as dressings, dips, and more.

The recipes provided below are roughly categorized by primary ingredient: grain-based, legume-based, tofu-based, or vegetable-based. Hopefully this schema will be useful for choosing which ones to make

TOPPING SAUCE RECIPES

USING GRAINS:

Each of the grains, or "grain-like seeds" in the case of quinoa and millet, are used for different purposes. Texture, nutritional content, sauce viscosity, convenience when cooking from scratch --- these are all impacted by what grain is being incorporated into the topping sauce. Barley is most likely the oldest grain we know that humans have consumed going back some 10,000 years! It's also a major player in these sauces for its thickening action (just as it is in soups and stews). Pearl barley, although a tad less nutritious than hulled barley, has the additional advantage of cooking up in around 30 minutes.

Millet, admittedly, is a favorite for making these sauces. Incredibly nutritious (the most alkaline of the grains), it's a real powerhouse. It's inexpensive and cooks up in 20 minutes. Millet can be cooked while the bread machine is working on the dough. Millet also has a fine thickening tendency and a lighter "taste feel" than barley.

Rolled oats are well known to be heart healthy and require no pre-preparation. Use non-instant old fashioned rolled oats. If you prefer to eat gluten-free, be sure to get oats that are certified to be "wheat contamination free," as cross-contamination does sometimes occur with wheat depending upon the manufacturer's facilities. Oats are not pre-cooked in these recipes.

Quinoa is also one of the oldest grains known and another nutritional winner, especially on the protein side of matters. Although it's a bit more expensive than the other grains, it does have the advantage of cooking up in 20 minutes. Quinoa offers a most delicate texture to a topping sauce. Both red and white quinoa can be used interchangeably, with the white version providing a more satisfactory beige appearance.

Rice is well known to most people, and in these recipes, short, long, white, and brown rice can be used interchangeably. Be sure not to use instant rice, but only unenriched. Rice promotes a bit more delicate taste than barley, but not as much as quinoa. It's advantages are price and availability. A disadvantage is the 40 minutes or so it takes to cook, although using a pressure cooker will bring that time down to around 15 minutes. When cooking a meal with rice on a given night, make extra, and then use what's leftover for a pizza (or different meal) in a few days.

There's more information about how to cook the above grains in Appendix 4.

Note: when using cooked grains, blending or processing times tend to be a bit longer and more vigorous towards the end to "smoothen" any graininess in the batter.

BARLEY-BASED RECIPES:

Barley and Almonds Sauce

INGREDIENTS:
- 1/2 cup pearl barley
- 1 1/2 cup water
- 1/3 cup sliced almonds
- 2 T. nutritional yeast
- 2 T. corn starch
- 1/2 t. salt (optional)

- 1/2 T. wet mustard
- 1 1/4 cups water

METHOD:

1. Bring water and barley to a boil, turn down to very low, simmer, cover, for 30 to 40 minutes (or until water has been absorbed). Let cool to room temperature.
2. Add all ingredients, except almonds and water, to blender or food processor (preferred). Add 3/4 cup of the water, start processing. Stop occasionally to add more nuts and water incrementally to blend until it's a smooth pancake-like batter.
3. This needs a long blend due to the high fiber of the barley and the skin on the almonds.

VARIATIONS:

- This sauce was originally made for a very spicy pizza (the filling ingredients had a lot of heat). Some cooks might prefer to add some spices or garlic powder to give it more kick. Paprika, garlic powder or chili powder would all work well.
- Substitute 1/4 cup of raw walnut pieces or raw cashews for the sliced almonds, adding another T. of corn starch to the blending.
- Omit salt, and add 2 T. blonde miso when blending.

NOTE:

- This recipe makes about 3 cups of sauce.

Barley, White Beans, and Horseradish Sauce

INGREDIENTS:

- 1/3 cup pearl barley
- 1 1/4 cup water
- 1 cup cooked white beans
- 2 T. corn starch
- 1/2 T. prepared horseradish
- 1/2 T. wet mustard
- 3/4 cup water

METHOD:

1. Rinse and drain the beans (to remove any salt).
2. Bring 1 1/4 cup water and barley to a boil, cover, turn down to very low, simmer, covered, for 30 to 40 minutes or less (until the water is absorbed). Let cool to room temperature.
3. Add all ingredients except the water to a blender or food processor, pulse a few times, and add half the water, pulse, and then the remaining water to blend until it's a smooth pancake-like batter.

NOTE:

• Makes enough sauce for two 12 to 14" inch pizzas (around 3 cups).

Barley, Carrot, and Potato Sauce

INGREDIENTS:

• 1/3 cup pearl barley
• 1/4 cup carrots (cut in 1/4" dice)
• 1 cup raw potato (peeled, cut in 1/4" dice)
• 1 3/4 cup water
• 1/2 cup water
• 2 T. corn starch
• 1 garlic clove (chopped)
• 1/2 t. red Tabasco sauce

METHOD:

1. Bring barley, carrots, potato, and 1 3/4 cup water to a boil, cover, turn heat down low, simmer about 30 to 45 minutes (until barley is tender). Let cool to room temperature. If necessary, drain.
2. Blend vegetable mixture and remaining ingredients together in a blender or food processor until the sauce is a smooth pancake-like batter.

NOTE:

• This very thick sauce is enough for two 12" to 14" pizzas (around 3 cups). It is visually interesting to pour small amounts of it as small mounds or clumps on the pizza (not unlike pieces of mozzarella on a conventional pie). From a color aspect, this sauce resembles cheddar cheese.

Barley, Carrot, Sunflower Seeds, and Chili Garlic Sauce

INGREDIENTS:
- 1 cup cooked pearl barley
- 1/2 cup carrots (1/4" crosswise slices)
- 1/4 cup raw sunflower seeds
- 2 1/2 T. Ener-G (see Glossary (p. 135))
- 1 T. chili garlic sauce (to taste)
- 1 cup water

METHOD:
1. Soak sunflower seeds in water 2 to 4 hours (or overnight, drain, store in refrigerator until using).
2. Cover carrots with water (not the 1 cup used later) in a sauce pan, bring to slow boil, cover, turn heat down very low, and simmer for a few minutes until fork tender. Drain, reserving any leftover liquid. The drained liquid can be used as part of the blending. Let the carrots cool to room temperature.
3. Blend all ingredients slowly at first, adding water as needed in 1/4 cup increments, until the sauce is a smooth and thick pancake-like batter. This takes longer than normal due to the fiber content of the barley.

NOTES:
- This makes around 3 cups, with 1 cup usually being the amount used on a 12 to 14" pizza.
- Leftover sauce is great with pasta, grains, or even in plant-based sushi maki rolls.

Barley, Mushrooms, and Tofu Sauce

INGREDIENTS:
- 1/3 cup pearl barley
- 1/2 cup mushrooms (chopped)
- 2/3 cup water

- 1/3 cup tofu
- 2 T. flax seeds
- 2 cloves garlic
- 1 to 1 1/2 T. wet mustard (to taste)
- 1/4 t. red Tabasco sauce (to taste)
- 1 cup water

METHOD:

1. Grind flax seeds in a spice mill.
2. Bring barley, mushrooms, and 2/3 cup water to a boil. Cover, turn heat down very low and simmer 30 to 40 minutes or until barley is done (don't worry if there's a little liquid still left over). Let cool and drain (if necessary).
3. Blend ingredients slowly at first, adding water as needed in 1/4 cup increments, until the sauce is a smooth and thick pancake batter-like sauce. This takes longer than normal due to the fiber content of the barley.

VARIATIONS:

- Mix chopped raw spinach into fully blended sauce.
- Experiment with different mustards: Dijon, Spice Brown, Stone Ground, and Classic mustard provide unique additions to the sauce's flavor profile.

NOTES:

- If using on spicy pizza fillings, for example, kim chi, omit the Tabasco sauce and use 1/2 t. dry mustard instead of wet mustard. The tofu in this topping sauce will contrast nicely with the pizza's "heat."
- This makes enough for two 12" to 14" pizzas (around 3 cups).

Barley, Cauliflower, and Vermouth Sauce

INGREDIENTS:

- 1 cup cauliflower (chopped)
- 1 cup cooked barley
- 1/4 cup sliced blanched almonds
- 1 T. dried tarragon (to taste)
- 2 T. corn starch
- 1 T. nutritional yeast

- 1/4 cup dry white vermouth (to taste)
- 3/4 cup water

METHOD:
1. Cover cauliflower with water, bring to a boil, cover, simmer for a few minutes until fork tender. Let cool to room temperature. Drain, reserving any leftover water if desired.
2. Add all ingredients, except almonds and water, to blender or food processor (preferred). Pulse a few times. Add 1/2 cup of the water, start processing. Stop occasionally and add more nuts and water incrementally until the mixture is a smooth and thick pancake-like batter.

VARIATIONS:
- Substitute some of the cauliflower with sliced carrots.
- Sprinkle some red chili pepper flakes and/or dried oregano on top of the sauce after it's on the pizza and ready for baking.
- Add a 2nd tablespoon of nutritional yeast and a tablespoon of wet mustard (Dijon mustard synergizes well with the Vermouth and tarragon).

NOTE:
- This makes enough for two 12" to 14" pizzas.

MILLET-BASED RECIPES:

Millet, Avocado, and Oregano Sauce

INGREDIENTS:
- 1 cup cooked millet
- 1/4 cup avocado (peeled, chopped)
- 1 T. lemon juice
- 2 T. corn starch
- 1 T. wet mustard (optional)
- 1 t. ground oregano
- 1 cup water

METHOD:

1. Blend all ingredients in a blender or food processor, adding water slowly between pulses. Blend until the sauce is a thick and smooth pancake-like batter. Processing may take longer than normal depending upon the firmness of the cooked millet.

NOTE:

- Makes enough sauce for two 12" to 14" pizzas (around 2 1/4 cups).

Millet, Black-eyed Peas, and Ginger Sauce

INGREDIENTS:

- 1 cup cooked millet
- 1 cup cooked black-eyed peas
- 1 1/2 t. ground ginger
- 2 T. corn starch
- 1/4 t. red Tabasco sauce (to taste)
- 1 T. wet mustard
- 1 T. nutritional yeast
- 1 1/4 cup water

METHOD:

1. Rinse and drain the beans (to remove any salt).
2. Pulse the beans a few times in a blender or food processor.
3. Process everything in a blender or food processor until the sauce is a smooth, thick pancake-like batter. Adding the water slowly in small increments will help in assessing the proper viscosity of the sauce.

NOTE:

- Makes enough for two 12" to 14" pizzas or one very large pizza (around 3 cups).

Millet, Cashews, and Mustard Sauce

INGREDIENTS:

- 2 cups cooked millet
- 1/3 cup cashews
- 2 T. nutritional yeast
- 1 t. garlic powder
- 1 t. salt (optional)
- 3 T. corn starch
- 1/2 T. wet mustard
- 1 3/4 to 2 cups water

METHOD:

1. Process everything in a blender or food processor until the mixture is a smooth, thick pancake-like batter. Adding the water incrementally will help facilitate assessing the sauce's thickness as it's blending.
2. This is a longer processing due to amount of millet.

NOTES:

- Using 1 3/4 cups of water yields a very thick sauce that makes nice "clumps" on top of a pizza, whereas more water will enable it to be poured easier from processing container.
- This makes around 3 cups of sauce.

Millet, Oats, and Cashews Sauce

INGREDIENTS:

- 1/2 cup millet (or 1 1/2 cups cooked)
- 1/2 cup rolled oats
- 1/4 cup whole raw cashews
- 2 T. nutritional yeast
- 2 1/2 T. corn starch
- 1/2 T. wet mustard
- 2 cups water

METHOD:

1. Bring millet and 1 cup of water to boil. Cover, turn heat down low, let simmer for 15 to 20 minutes. This yields 1 1/2 cup cooked millet. Let cool to room temperature.
2. Blend all ingredients pulsing frequently at the start, adding the nuts and water incrementally to get a smooth and thick pancake-like batter.

NOTE:

- This recipe makes enough topping sauce for two 12" or 14" pizzas.

Millet, Quinoa, and Flax Seeds Sauce

INGREDIENTS:

- 1 cup cooked millet
- 1 cup cooked white quinoa
- 1/4 c. blanched sliced almonds
- 1 T. nutritional yeast
- 2 T. flax seeds
- 2 T. cumin seeds
- 1 T. wet mustard
- 2 1/2 T. corn starch
- 1/2 t. red Tabasco sauce (to taste)
- 1/4 t. garlic powder
- 1 3/4 c. water

METHOD:

1. Grind flax seeds and cumin seeds in a spice mill.
2. Add all ingredients but the nuts and water to blender or food processor. Pulse a few times, gradually adding more water and nuts into you get the mixture to a point where it can be blended on medium high for a smooth pancake-like batter consistency.

VARIATION:

- Roast cumin seeds under the broiler until dark before grinding.

NOTE:

- Makes enough for two 12 to 14" pizza (around 3 cups of sauce).

Millet, Sunflower Seeds, and Oregano Sauce

INGREDIENTS:

- 1 cup cooked millet
- 1/4 cup raw sunflower seeds
- 1/4 cup nutritional yeast
- 2 T. corn starch
- 2 T. dried crushed oregano
- 1 cup water

METHOD:

1. Add all ingredients but nuts and water to blender or food processor. Pulse a few times, gradually adding more water and nuts until the mixture can be processed into a smooth and thick pancake batter-like consistency.

NOTES:

- This recipe makes a very thick sauce. As blobs on top of the pizza, it is reminiscent of raw mozzarella slices on a Margherita-style pizza. Works well for one 12" to 14" pizza.
- Soaking the sunflower seeds for 2 to 4 hours, then draining, will make the sauce a bit more fluffy in texture.

Sprouted Millet, Flax Seeds, and Cashews

INGREDIENTS:

- 1 cup millet
- 1/4 cup flax seeds
- 1/4 cup raw cashews
- 1 1/2 T. ground cumin
- 1 T. nutritional yeast
- ground black pepper
- pinch of salt (optional)
- 1 cup water

METHOD:

1. Soak millet and flax seed separately in equal amounts of water overnight; drain next morning. Let sit in a covered strainer or colander until it's time for dinner.

2. If the weather is warm (and your kitchen is too), you may need to rinse and drain the millet and flax seed again mid-day.

3. When ready to make the sauce, blend all ingredients together, adding the raw cashews and liquid slowly, until the sauce is a smooth and thick pancake batter-like consistency. This recipe needs a longer processing then most due to the flax seeds.

VARIATION:

- Soak the cashews overnight or for at least 2 hours, drain, put in covered bowl until ready to use.

NOTE:

- Makes around 2 1/2 cups of sauce.

Millet, Sprouted Sunflower Seeds and Dijon Mustard

INGREDIENTS:

- 1 cup cooked millet
- 1/2 cup of sunflower seeds
- 2 T. corn starch
- 2 T. nutritional yeast
- 1 1/2 T. Dijon mustard (to taste)
- 1 to 1 1/4 cups water

METHOD:

1. Soak the sunflower seeds in water overnight, drain, keep in covered strainer or colander until ready to use later in the day.

2. Blend all ingredients together, adding the sunflower seeds and liquid slowly, until the sauce is a thick smooth pancake-like batter.

VARIATIONS:

- For thicker sauce, try using 1 cup of water. Add the water slowly during processing to gauge the viscosity of the sauce.
- This recipe was designed to be more towards a base mozzarella in taste, so some Heart Healthy Pizza cooks might prefer to add some additional herbs (fresh or dried) or spices after the sauce has been initially processed.
- Sunflower seeds can be used the next day if they are rinsed around dinner time, and left out over night. In the morning, rinse, strain, keep the sunflower seeds in a colander until ready to make pizza, and if the weather is warm or they are getting very dry, rinse them again mid-day.
- If pressed for time, soak seeds for 2 to 4 hours, drain.
- Use 1/3 to 1/2 cup of raw, unsoaked walnuts in place of the sunflower seeds and a Spicy Brown mustard instead of Dijon mustard.

NOTE:

- This makes enough for one 12" to 14" pizza, two if you use 1 1/4 cups of water.

OAT-BASED RECIPES:

Oats, Mustard, and Nutritional Yeast Sauce

INGREDIENTS:

- 1 cup rolled oats
- 1 T. nutritional yeast
- 1/2 t. garlic powder (optional)
- 1/2 t. onion powder (optional)
- 1/2 t. paprika (optional)
- 1 T. wet mustard
- 1 t. lemon juice
- 2 T. corn starch
- 3/4 cup water

METHOD:

1. Add all ingredients to blender or food processor reserving the water. Pulse the mixture a few times, and gradually increase processing speed while slowly adding small amounts of the water. Blend until it's a smooth and thick pancake-like batter.

NOTE:

- Makes around 1 cup of sauce.

Oats, Cannellini Beans, and Garlic Sauce

INGREDIENTS:

- 1 cup rolled oats
- 1 15 oz. can cannellini beans (white kidney beans)
- 2 cloves garlic (chopped)
- 2 T. Ener-G
- 1 to 2 T. nutritional yeast
- 1 t. paprika (optional)
- 1 1/4 to 1 1/2 cups water

METHOD:

1. Rinse and drain beans (to remove salt).
2. Blend, starting first with the beans only, pulsing a few times, then adding the rest of the ingredients, reserving the water to add slowly while increasing the processing speed and gauging the thickness of the batter until it's a smooth and thick pancake-like batter.

NOTES:

- This recipe is a bit bland, having been designed on purpose for use on a tri-color peppers and hot chili pepper flakes pizza. You may want to spice or herb it up a bit, depending upon your anticipated pizza fillings. A little chili powder, red Tabasco sauce, or paprika will liven it up.
- Makes around 3 cups of sauce (for two 1 lb. pizzas, 12" to 14").

Oats, Cauliflower, and Carrot Sauce

INGREDIENTS:

- 1 cup rolled oats
- 1 cup chopped raw cauliflowerets
- 1/2 cup chopped raw carrots (1/4")
- 2 T. Ener-G
- 1 t. dry mustard
- 1 T. nutritional yeast
- 1/3 cup white wine
- 1 1/3 cups water

METHOD:

1. Cover cauliflower and carrots in pot with water.
2. Bring to boil and simmer until tender. Drain, let cool to room temperature.
3. Put everything into a blender or food processor, pulse a few times, start the blend and add water incrementally until the sauce is a smooth pancake-like batter. Additional water might be needed depending upon the cut and subsequent measurement of the vegetables.

NOTE:

- Makes around 3 cups of sauce.

Oats, Carrot, and Corn Sauce

INGREDIENTS:

- 1 cup rolled oats
- 1 medium carrot (diced, about 3/4 cup)
- 1/2 cup water
- 1 t. dried oregano
- 1/2 cup cooked corn kernels (rinsed and drained if canned)
- 1/2 t. dry mustard
- 2 T. flax seeds
- 1 T. lime juice
- 1 1/2 cup of water

METHOD:
1. Grind flax seeds in a spice mill.
2. Rinse and/or drain the corn as needed.
3. Put diced carrot, water, and oregano into small pot. Bring to a boil, then simmer covered on very low until fork tender. Drain (reserve liquid if you want to use elsewhere) and let come to room temperature.
4. Add everything into a blender or food processor, adding the 1 1/2 cups of liquid (water) around 1/4 cup at a time, blending carefully until it's a smooth pancake-like batter.

NOTES:
- Using frozen corn isn't advised, but if need be, rinse and drain. Use 1/4 cup (or more) less water.
- Makes around 3 cups of sauce.

Oats, Pinto Beans, and Salsa Sauce

INGREDIENT:
- 1 cup rolled oats
- 1 15 oz. can pinto beans
- 1 to 2 T. nutritional yeast
- 3 T. Ener-G (or 2 T. corn starch)
- 4 T. of red salsa (store bought or Red Tomato Salsa (p. 27))
- 1 1/4 to 1 1/2 cups of water

METHOD:
1. Rinse and drain the beans (to remove salt).
2. Blend starting first with the beans only, pulsing a few times, then adding the rest of the ingredients, reserving the water to add slowly as the processing speed is increased and a smooth, thick pancake-like batter is achieved.

NOTES:
- Some salsas are chunky, some are less so. If using chunky and there's a lot of water, drain before adding to mixture. If using a smoother salsa, less water might be needed.

- The heat in homemade or purchased salsa varies considerably, and adjusting the spice levels of the sauce during blending, to taste, might be necessary. Chili powder, red Tabasco sauce, and cayenne pepper could be used.
- Another approach is to sprinkle any of these spices (including paprika) or red chili pepper flakes on the pizza after the sauce has been added.
- Makes around 3 cups of sauce.

QUINOA-BASED RECIPES:

Quinoa, Artichoke Hearts, and Dijon Mustard Sauce

INGREDIENTS:
- 14 oz. can of water-packed artichoke hearts (about 1 1/4 cups quartered)
- 1 cup cooked white quinoa
- 1 T. lemon juice
- 1 T. Dijon mustard
- 2 1/2 T. corn starch
- 1 1/4 cup water

METHOD:
1. Drain artichokes (leftover liquid can be used in salad dressings, soups, or sauces). Chop up the artichoke hearts into 1/2" pieces (cut lengthwise, then cross-cut).
2. Put all ingredients in a blender or food processor. Start slow with pulsing and gradually increase speed. Blend long and hard until the mixture is a smooth pancake-like batter.

VARIATION:
- Sprinkle the topping sauce with paprika before baking.

NOTE:
- This recipe makes a very delicate sauce, suitable for two 12" to 14" pizzas.

Quinoa, Artichoke Hearts, and Sunflower Seeds Sauce

INGREDIENTS:

- 1 14 oz. can water-packed artichokes
- 1 cup cooked white quinoa
- 1/2 cup raw sunflower seeds
- 2 T. lemon juice
- 2 T. wet mustard
- 2 T. corn starch
- 2 1/2 cups water

METHOD:

1. Drain artichokes. Chop up the artichoke hearts into 1/2" pieces (cut lengthwise, then cross-cut).
2. Soak sunflower seeds in water all day, at least 2 to 4 hours, until ready to use. Drain.
3. Put all ingredients in a blender or food processor, pulse a few times, add some of the water, pulse a few more times. Gradually add water and start blending the mixture, gradually increasing speed until it's a very smooth pancake-like batter.

VARIATION:

- Add 2 T. prepared horseradish while blending.

NOTE:

- Makes around 4 cups of sauce.

Quinoa, Carrots, and Corn Sauce

INGREDIENTS:

- 1/2 cup uncooked white quinoa
- 1/2 cup chopped carrots
- 1/2 T. red chili pepper flakes
- 1/2 cup drained corn (not frozen)
- 1 t. garlic powder
- 1 T. wet mustard

- 3 T. flax seeds
- pinch salt (optional)
- 1 1/4 to 1 1/2 cup water

METHOD:
1. Grind flax seeds in spice mill.
2. Rinse and drain corn (if packed with salt).
3. Cook quinoa, carrots, pepper flakes, in 1 cup water. Bring to boil, cover, and simmer on very low for 15 to 20 minutes. Let cool to room temperature.
4. Blend together all ingredients in food processor or blender with remaining water. This requires a longer processing time than normal because of the flax seeds.

NOTES:
- Using frozen corn isn't advised, but if need be, rinse and drain. Use 1/4 cup (or more) less water.
- This is a fluffy sauce with some nutty undertones from the flax seeds.
- This recipe makes approximately 3 cups of sauce.

Quinoa, Cauliflower, Almonds, and Garlic Sauce

INGREDIENTS:
- 1/3 cup uncooked white quinoa
- 1 cup chopped raw cauliflower (1/4 to 1/2")
- 1 1/2 cup water
- 2 T. Ener-G
- 1/3 cup blanched slivered almonds
- juice of one medium lemon (2 to 3 T.)
- 3 cloves garlic (peeled, chopped)
- 2 T. nutritional yeast
- 2/3 cup water

METHOD:
1. Bring quinoa, cauliflower and water in a pot to boil, cover, and then simmer on very low until done (about 20 minutes). Let cool to room temperature.

2. Put all ingredients (including undrained vegetable mixture) except water and nuts into a food processor (preferred) or blender.

3. Pulse the machine a few times, then gradually add water and the nuts in small amounts, slowly increasing processing speed until it's a smooth pancake-like batter.

4. This is a long blend to make sure the garlic is liquefied.

NOTES:

- A very "fluffy" sauce that works best as blotches or in a lattice pattern on top of the pizza.
- Makes enough sauce for two 12" to 14" pizzas.

Quinoa and Colored Sweet Peppers Sauce

INGREDIENTS:

- 1/3 cup quinoa
- 2/3 cup water
- 1 cup chopped colored sweet peppers (red, yellow, orange as desired)
- 2 T. lemon or lime juice
- 2 t. ground ginger
- 1 T. wet mustard
- 2 T. corn starch
- 1 T. flax seeds
- 1 lg. garlic clove
- 1/2 t. red Tabasco sauce (to taste)
- 1/2 to 1 cup water

METHOD:

1. Grind flax seeds in a spice mill.

2. Combine quinoa and water in pot, bring to a boil, cover, and turn heat very low to simmer for about 20 minutes (until water is gone). Remove from heat, and let cool, covered, until at room temperature. Use a fork to fluff up the quinoa mixture.

3. Blend all remaining ingredients and cooked quinoa together, adding the water in small increments until the mixture is a thick, smooth pancake-like batter. This recipe will take longer than normal due to the flax seeds.

NOTE:

- Makes enough sauce for two 12" to 14" pizzas.

Quinoa, Lima Beans, and Walnuts Sauce

INGREDIENTS:

- 1 cup cooked white quinoa
- 2/3 cup cooked large lima beans
- 1/3 cup chopped walnuts
- 3 T. corn starch
- 1 T. nutritional yeast
- ground pepper (to taste)
- 1/2 T. red Tabasco sauce (to taste)
- 1 t. garlic powder
- 1 1/4 cup water

METHOD:

1. Rinse and drain beans (to remove salt if from a can).
2. Put everything but water and nuts into a blender of food processor (preferred). Use some slow quick pulses at first, then gradually increase processing speed while slowly adding water and nuts until the mixture is a smooth and thick pancake-like batter.

NOTE:

- Makes about 3 cups of sauce.

Quinoa, Sweet Potato, and Corn Sauce

INGREDIENTS:

- 1/2 cup uncooked white quinoa
- 1/2 sweet potato (peeled & grated, about 1 cup total)
- 1 1/4 cup water
- 1/2 cup corn kernels (if canned, rinsed, drained)
- 2 T. Energ-G
- 1 t. red Tabasco sauce (or to taste)

- 1 1/2 T. Chipolte mustard (or flavor of choice)
- 3/4 to 1 cup water

METHOD:

1. Put quinoa and sweet potato into pot with water. Bring to boil, cover, let simmer for 20 minutes (until the water is gone). Turn off heat and let sit for 5 minutes (still covered). Uncover, let cool to room temperature.
2. Add quinoa & sweet potato mixture to blender or food processor (preferred). Pulse the mixture a few times.
3. Add rest of the ingredients, with the water added in between pulse blends, gradually increasing processing until a smooth pancake-like batter is achieved.

NOTES:

- The Chipolte mustard adds a nice kick in taste. The overall taste may have to be adjusted a bit if using a different mustard.
- Using frozen corn is not advised.
- Makes near 3 cups of sauce.

Quinoa, Tofu, and Flax Seeds Sauce

INGREDIENTS:

- 1 cup cooked white quinoa
- 1/2 cup tofu (lite extra-firm preferred)
- 2 T. flax seeds
- 2 T. corn starch
- 1 t. garlic powder
- 1 t. onion powder
- 1 1/2 T. Dijon mustard
- 1 to 1 1/4 cups water

METHOD:

1. Grind flax seeds in a spice mill.
2. Put cooked quinoa in blender or food processor, followed by the rest of the ingredients. Pulse a few times, gradually increasing processing speed and adding water incrementally until the mixture is a smooth, thick pancake-

like batter (due to amount of grain, this might take longer than usual).

NOTE:
- Makes approximately 2 cups of sauce, enough for two 12 to 14" pizzas.

RICE-BASED RECIPES:

Rice, Cannellini Beans, and Almonds Sauce

INGREDIENTS:
- 1 cup cooked rice (long-grain brown works well)
- 1/4 cup slivered blanched almonds
- 1 t. dry mustard
- 2 medium cloves of garlic (peeled and chopped)
- 2/3 cup cannellini beans (drained and rinsed)
- 1 T. nutritional yeast
- 1 T. flax seeds
- 1 T. Ener-G
- 1/4 t. red Tabasco sauce to taste (optional)
- 3 t. blonde or white miso
- 1 cup water

METHOD:
1. Rinse and drain beans (to remove any salt).
2. Grind flax seeds in a spice mill.
3. Add ingredients starting with beans and rice. Pulse a few times in a blender or food processor. Add the rest of the ingredients except the water and nuts, pulse a few times.
4. Gradually add the water and nuts, increasing processing speed until it's a smooth and thick pancake-like batter.

VARIATION:
- Substitute cannellini beans (white kidney beans) with navy beans or great northern beans.

- This recipe makes enough topping sauce for a two 12" to 14" pizzas or one large one (from 2 lbs. of dough), approximately 3 cups.

Rice and Cauliflower Sauce

INGREDIENTS:

- 1 cup cooked long grain brown rice
- 1 cup chopped cauliflower (1/2")
- 1 T. of dried oregano
- 3 T. nutritional yeast
- 3 T. corn starch
- 1 cup water

METHOD:

1. Cover cauliflower with water in a pot, bring to a boil, cover, and turn heat down low to simmer a few minutes until fork tender. Let drain, let cool to room temperature.
2. Put 1st two ingredients into a blender or food processor, pulse a few times. Add the rest of ingredients, begin with slow processing, gradually increasing speed until it's a smooth pancake-like batter.

NOTE:

- This recipe makes approximately 2 1/2 cups of sauce, sufficient for two 12" to 14" pizzas or one large one (from 2 lbs. of dough).

Rice, Oats, and Cashews Sauce

INGREDIENTS:

- 1/2 cup cooked brown rice
- 1/2 cup rolled oats
- 1/3 cup raw cashews
- 3 T. corn starch
- 1 t. salt (optional)
- 1 T. lemon juice
- 2 T. wet mustard

• 1 1/2 cups water

METHOD:

1. If desired, cashews can be soaked overnight, drained and stored in the morning.
2. Put rice, oats, and 1/2 cup of the water into a blender or food processor. Pulse a few times. Add the water and nuts incrementally, gradually increasing the processing speed. Add the other ingredients and blend until it's a smooth and thick pancake-like batter.

NOTE:

• This recipe makes about 2 1/4 cups of sauce, enough for two 12" to 14" pizzas.

Rice and Sunflower Seeds Sauce

INGREDIENTS:

• 1 cup cooked long grain brown rice
• 1/3 cup raw sunflower seeds
• 2 T. nutritional yeast
• 1 t. garlic powder
• 1 t. onion powder
• 1/2 t. paprika
• 3 T. corn starch
• 1 1/4 cup water

METHOD:

1. Soak sunflower seeds overnight. Drain and store covered in a small bowl in refrigerator.
2. Pulse the rice and sunflower seeds a few times in a blender or food processor. Add the rest of the ingredients, gradually increasing the processing speed and adding water in small amounts until the mixture is a smooth and thick pancake-like batter.

VARIATION:

• Add spices or herbs (fresh or dried) of choice after blending, and mix with a large wooden spoon. Italian seasonings works well as does some chopped fresh basil.

NOTE:
- This recipe makes enough for two 12" to 14" pizzas with some leftover.

Rice, Chickpeas, and Corn Sauce

INGREDIENTS:
- 1/2 cup cooked chickpeas
- 1/2 cup cooked brown rice
- 1/2 cup corn (drained if from can)
- 1 T. nutritional yeast
- 1/2 t. garlic powder
- 2 T. corn starch
- 3/4 cups water

METHOD:
1. Rinse and drain chickpeas (to remove any salt).
2. Put the rice and chickpeas in a blender or food processor and pulse a few times. Add remaining ingredients and process, gradually increasing speed until it's a thick pancake-like batter.

VARIATION:
- Depending upon how spicy your pizza filling is, you may consider adding a little more "heat" when blending the sauce, such as cayenne pepper.
- Add chopped peppers and/or black olives after processing.

NOTES:
- If using frozen corn (not recommended), be sure to rinse and drain, let come to room temperature. Start with 1/4 cup of water, adding a bit more slowly so viscosity can be gauged (less water will be needed).
- This recipe makes about 2 cups of sauce.

LEGUME-BASED RECIPES:

Cooked legumes provide not only a unique taste to these sauces, but also a velvety almost parmesan-like texture. Another benefit in using beans is the amount of fiber and nutrition they bring to the topping sauces. Both canned and home cooked beans have been used in testing these recipes. For the latter, cook in advance, drain, and store in plastic bags in the freezer. They can be thawed out very quickly by putting the bag of beans in warm water or by rinsing the frozen beans in a colander.

A "crockette," a small slow cooker, is very useful to slowly cook beans over the course of a day, while some people prefer the speed and efficiency of using a pressure cooker. If not cooked sufficiently, home-cooked beans won't be tender enough for these sauces, whereas canned beans are quite soft and easily processed smoothly. Canned beans have the advantage of being very quick. Be sure to not only drain them (unless the recipe calls for otherwise), but also to rinse them off to get rid of extra salt. There's more information about how to cook beans in Appendix 4.

For the following recipes, cannellini beans (white kidney beans), great northern beans, white beans, and navy beans can be used pretty much interchangeably. Note: 1 15 oz. can of beans equals about 1 1/2 to 1 2/3 cups of drained beans, depending upon the size of the bean.

Chickpeas, Oats, and Pimentos Sauce

INGREDIENTS:

- 1 15 oz. can chickpeas
- 1 cup rolled oats
- 1 2 oz. jar pimentos (drained)
- 3 T. flax seeds
- 1 1/2 t. garlic powder
- 2 T. wet mustard of choice
- 1/2 t. paprika
- 1/2 t. red Tabasco sauce
- 1/4 t. salt (optional)
- 1 1/2 to 2 cups water

METHOD:

1. Rinse and drain beans (to remove any salt).
2. Grind flax seeds in a spice mill.
3. Add oats and beans to a blender or food processor and pulse a few times.
4. Add the rest of the ingredients and some of the water. Pulse a few more times, adding water incrementally to gauge viscosity, then process until it's a smooth and thick pancake-like batter.

NOTES:

- Depending upon how packed the oats are, the additional 1/2 cup of water might be needed.
- Makes around 3 cups of topping sauce.

Lima Beans, Millet, and Flax Seed Sauce

INGREDIENTS:

- 1 cup cooked lima beans
- 1/2 cup cooked millet
- 2 T. flax seeds
- 2 - 3 cloves of garlic (peeled and chopped)
- 1 1/2 T. dried oregano
- 1 T. nutritional yeast

- 1 cup water

METHOD:

1. **1.** Rinse and drain beans (to remove salt).
2. **2.** Grind flax seeds in a spice mill.
3. **3.** Add lima beans and millet to a blender or food processor and pulse a few times.
4. **4.** Add the rest of the ingredients and some of the water. Pulse a few more times, slowly adding water, then processing until it's a smooth and thick pancake-like batter.

VARIATIONS:

- Use 1/2 cup of water with 1/2 cup of a strong white wine (such as a Chardonnay).
- Use dried tarragon instead of oregano, substituting some of the water with white vermouth (careful! vermouth has a strong taste).

NOTES:

- This is very thick sauce and a spatula might be needed to smooth it on top of the pizza crust. If using this as a sauce on top of fillings, add a little bit more water to make it easier to pour.
- Makes approximately 2 1/2 cups of sauce.

Navy Beans, Rice, and Fresh Basil Sauce

INGREDIENTS:

- 1 15 oz. can navy beans (drained and rinsed)
- 1 cup cooked brown rice
- 3 T. corn starch
- 2 T. nutritional yeast
- 1 clove garlic (peeled and chopped)
- 2 T. lemon juice
- 1 T. ground flax seeds
- 1 1/2 cup chopped fresh basil
- 1/2 t. ground black pepper (or to taste)
- 2 cups water

METHOD:

1. Rinse and drain beans (to remove salt).
2. Add navy beans and rice to a blender or food processor and pulse a few times.
3. Add the rest of the ingredients and some of the water. Pulse a few more times, adding water, gauging the viscosity (due to variations in measuring fresh basil), and process until it's a smooth and thick pancake-like batter.

NOTE:

• Makes over 3 cups of sauce.

Great Northern Beans, Millet, and Cashew Sauce

INGREDIENTS:

• 1 15 oz. can of great northern beans
• 1/2 cup cooked millet
• 1/4 cup cashews
• 3 T. corn starch
• 1/4 t. ground black pepper
• 1/2 t. dry mustard (or 1. T wet mustard)
• 1/2 t paprika
• 1 3/4 cup water

METHOD:

1. Rinse and drain beans (to remove salt).
2. Add great northern beans and millet to a blender or food processor and pulse a few times.
3. Add the rest of the ingredients, then add some of the nuts and water. Pulse a few more times, adding the rest of the water and nuts, and processing until you have a smooth pancake-like batter.

NOTE:

• Makes about 3 cups, sufficient for two 12" to 14" pizzas (from 2 lbs. of dough)

White Beans and Millet Sauce

INGREDIENTS:

- 1 15 oz. can Great Northern Beans
- 1 cup cooked millet
- 2 T. corn starch
- 1 T. nutritional yeast
- 2 cups water

METHOD:

1. Rinse and drain beans (to remove salt).
2. Add beans and millet to blender or food processor and pulse a few times. Add the rest of the ingredients, slowly adding the rest of the water incrementally, processing until it's a smooth and thick pancake-like batter.

NOTES:

- Although this recipe is similar to the preceding, the key differences are the amount of millet and that it was made deliberately bland to counteract an extremely hot and spicy homemade kim chi filling. You may want to add a bit more heat with various spices.
- Makes about 3 cups, sufficient for two 12" to 14" pizzas (from 2 lbs. of dough)

Cannellini Beans, Oregano, and Walnut Sauce

INGREDIENTS:

- 1 15 oz. can Cannellini beans (white kidney beans)
- 1/3 cup packed fresh chopped oregano
- 1/4 cup raw walnut bits
- 1/2 t. garlic powder
- 1 T. spicy brown mustard
- 2 T. corn starch
- 2 T. lemon juice
- 1/4 t. ground pepper
- 1/2 t. salt
- 3/4 cup water

METHOD:

    1. Rinse and drain beans (to remove salt).

    2. Add beans to a blender or food processor and pulse a few times. Add the rest of the ingredients, slowly adding the rest of the water, processing until it's a smooth and thick pancake-like batter.

NOTE:

- Makes enough for at least two 12" to 14" pizzas (from 2 lbs. of dough)

Navy Beans and Pecans Sauce

INGREDIENTS:

- 1 15 oz. can Navy Beans
- 2 T. nutritional yeast
- 1/3 cup pecan pieces
- 4 cloves garlic (peeled and chopped)
- 1 T. Stone-ground mustard
- 2 1/2 T. corn starch
- 2 T. lemon juice
- 3/4 cup water

METHOD:

    1. Rinse and drain beans (to remove salt).

    2. Add beans to a blender or food processor and pulse a few times. Add the rest of the ingredients, slowly adding the water and nuts, processing until it's a smooth and thick pancake-like batter.

    3. A longer processing time might be needed than normal due to skin of pecans.

NOTE:

- Makes enough for about two 12" to 14" pizzas (from 2 lbs. of dough)

Yellow Dal and Rice Sauce

INGREDIENTS:

- 1/2 cup yellow dal (see Glossary, p. 144)
- 1 to 2 cups of water (see Note)

- 1 cup cooked brown rice
- 1 t. garlic powder
- 2 t. curry powder
- 1/2 t. of salt (optional, to taste)
- 1 lemon (juiced)
- 3 T. corn starch
- 1 cup water

METHOD:

1. Rinse dal several times, picking out any small pebbles or non-yellow dal.
2. Bring dal and water to boil in a small pot, then turn heat to the lowest setting to simmer for around 30 minutes. Let sit 5 minutes, uncover, and let cool to room temperature. Drain.
3. Add 1 cup of the cooked dal and the rice to a blender or food processor. Pulse the mixture a few times.
4. Add the remaining ingredients, reserving the water to add slowly in small amounts as the processing speed is gradually increased. A long hard blending will make a very smooth pancake-like batter.

NOTES:

- Use enough water to cover the dal at least 1/2" (the amount will depend upon how wide and deep your cooking pot is, as well as the size of the dal).
- Makes approximately 2 cups of sauce.

TOFU-BASED RECIPES:

It wasn't until Tofutti Yogurt was available in the marketplace that most people knew anything about this wonderful soy product. Long used in Asia, tofu is somewhat ubiquitous these days, being found in many food products and in many different forms.

On the positive side, tofu's ability to pick up flavorings if cooked right is wonderful, and certainly the different textures of tofu make it a very versatile ingredient. Although a surprising number of people don't like tofu, many believe that's more from its "hippie food image" and probably not having it served to them in a truly tasty fashion.

On the negative side, tofu can contain a lot of fat per calories per serving. In the following recipes, regular extra firm tofu can be used, although "lite" extra firm or firm "Mori-Nu" packaged tofu is preferred, which can be stored outside the refrigerator for several months.

As a topping sauce, tofu firms well to a custard and unless spiced or herbed up, a more bland sauce that will contrast well with a pizza fillings that are high in heat and spice. Special attention should be paid as to how much water or liquid is added when processing. The water content of various types or brands of tofu will vary. For the following recipes, the tofu was not pressed, but just drained.

Tofu, Basil, and White Wine Sauce

INGREDIENTS:
- 1 box 12.3 oz. lite extra-firm Mori-Nu Tofu (preferred)
- 1 cup fresh basil (chopped)
- 1/4 cup sunflower seeds
- 1 T. lemon juice
- 1 T. wet mustard
- 2 T. corn starch
- 2 cloves garlic (peeled and chopped)
- 1/2 t. red chill pepper flakes (optional)
- pinch of salt (optional)
- 2/3 cup white wine (or water)
- 1/3 cup water

METHOD:

1. Add tofu and basil to a blender or food processor. Pulse a few times. Add remaining ingredients, pulse a few times.

2. Slowly add the white wine and water mixed together slowly while processing and gradually increasing speed until it's a smooth and thick pancake-like batter.

NOTES:

- This recipe works well on the crust of a pizza and "pressing" the vegetables lightly into the sauce a little bit.
- Makes enough for two 12" to 14" pizzas.

Tofu and Lemon Sauce

INGREDIENTS:

- 1 box lite extra-firm Mori-Nu Tofu (preferred)
- 1/4 cup lemon juice
- 2 T. nutritional yeast
- 1/2 paprika (optional)
- 2 T. corn starch
- pinch of salt (optional)
- 1/3 cup water

METHOD:

1. Add all ingredients to a blender or food processor. Pulse a few times, gradually increasing the speed of processing until it's a smooth and thick pancake-like batter.

NOTES:

- This is a good basic recipe that can be built upon by the creative Heart Healthy Pizza cook. It was originally made a tad bland to put over some very spicy fillings, but can easily be modified to taste by adding additional spices and/or dried herbs.
- Makes enough for 1 12" to 14" pizza.

Tofu and Rice Sauce

INGREDIENTS:

- 1 box lite extra-firm Mori-Nu Tofu (preferred)
- 1 cup cooked brown rice
- 3 T. corn starch
- 1/2 t. paprika
- 1 t. garlic powder
- 2 t. dry mustard
- 1/2 t. salt (optional)
- 1 T. nutritional yeast
- 1 to 1 1/2 cups water

METHOD:

1. Add tofu and brown rice to a blender or food processor. Pulse a few times.
2. Add remaining ingredients, slowly add portions of the water as you bring mixture to a full blend.
3. Process until it's a smooth and thick pancake-like batter, gauging the thickness carefully and using additional water if need be.

NOTE:

- This makes about 3 1/2 cups of a medium-thick custard-like sauce, suitable for two 12" to 14" pizzas (leftover sauce works well on cooked vegetables and with pasta).

Tofu and Millet Sauce

INGREDIENTS:

- 1 cup tofu (lite extra firm preferred)
- 1 cup cooked millet
- 1 T. lemon juice
- 1 T. wet mustard
- 1/2 t. paprika
- 1/2 t. onion powder
- 3 T. corn starch
- 1/2 T. nutritional yeast

- pinch of salt (optional)
- 1 cup water

METHOD:

1. Add tofu and millet to a blender or food processor, and pulse a few times.
2. Add remaining ingredients, reserving the water to add slowly as the mixture is being processed.
3. Gradually increase processing speed until it's a smooth and thick pancake-like batter.

NOTES:

- Rinse and drain beans (to remove salt). This makes a very thick 3 cups of sauce.
- Sprinkle paprika (to taste) on top of the sauce before cooking the assembled pizza.

Tofu, Millet, and Cocktail Sauce Sauce

INGREDIENTS:

- 1/2 box lite extra-firm Mori-Nu Tofu
- 1 cup cooked millet
- 3 T. corn starch
- 3 T. cocktail sauce
- 1/2 t. dry mustard
- 1 t. garlic powder
- 2 t. nutritional yeast
- 3/4 to 1 cup water

METHOD:

1. Add tofu and cooked millet to a blender or food processor. Pulse the mixture a few times.
2. Add remaining ingredients, reserving the water to add slowly as the mixture is being processed.
3. Gradually increase processing speed until it's a smooth and thick pancake-like batter.

NOTES:

- Recipe makes just under 3 cups of sauce with an interesting reddish-orange tint and delightful tang from the cocktail sauce.
- Some Cocktail Sauces contain "anchovies" so check the label before purchasing.
- A "quickie" Cocktail Sauce can be made by mixing a little lemon juice, prepared horseradish, ketchup (or tomato paste with some water) to taste.

Tofu, Dill, and Dijon Mustard Sauce

INGREDIENTS:

- 2 cups tofu (lite extra firm preferred)
- 1 T. lemon juice
- 1 T. Dijon mustard
- 1/2 T. dried dill (optional and to taste)
- 3 T. corn starch
- 1/2 cup water
- ground black pepper (to taste)

METHOD:

1. Add all ingredients to a blender or food processor (preferred) and pulse a few times. Add water slowly, gradually increase processing speed until the sauce is a smooth and thick pancake-like batter, adding more water if needed.

NOTE:

- Makes enough for at least two 12" to 14" pizzas (just under 3 cups of sauce).

Tofu and Sprouted Sunflower Seeds Sauce

INGREDIENTS:

- 1 cup tofu (lite extra firm preferred)
- 1/2 cup raw sunflower seeds
- 2 - 2 1/2 T. corn starch
- 3 T. nutritional yeast

- 1 1/2 t. ground cumin
- 1/2 t. drops red Tabasco sauce (to taste)
- 1/4 t. salt (optional)
- 1 cup water (see Notes)

METHOD:

1. Soak sunflower seeds overnight, drain and rinse the next morning. Let sit covered in colander or strainer covered, rinsing a couple of times during the day if they are getting try.
2. Use the sunflowers that evening, or the next day (being sure to rinse, drain in the evening, and a few times the next day).
3. Add tofu and sunflower seeds to blender or food processor and pulse a few times. Add remaining ingredients reserving the water to add slowly as you increase processing speed to make a smooth and thick pancake-like batter.

NOTES:

- Makes around 2 cups of sauce.
- The amount made will depend on how watery the tofu used is and how much water is used. Start with 3/4 cup of water at first.

VEGETABLE-BASED RECIPES:

Cauliflower, Carrots, and Black-eyed Peas Sauce

INGREDIENTS:

- 1 cup cauliflower (chopped, 1" max)
- 1 cup cooked black-eyed peas
- 1/3 cup carrots (peeled and chopped, 1/2" max)
- 1 T. wet mustard
- 1 to 2 cloves garlic (chopped)
- 2 T. Ener-G
- 1 1/4 cup liquid (left-over cooking broth and water)

METHOD:

1. Rinse and drain black-eyed peas (to remove any salt).

2. Cover cauliflower & carrots with water, bring to a boil, simmer for a few minutes until fork tender. Drain, reserving left-over liquid (broth), and let both liquid and vegetables cool.

3. Put vegetables and half the liquid into a blender or processor, pulsing a few times. Add remaining ingredients, pulse a few times adding the last of the water/broth slowly as the processing speed is increased and the sauce is a smooth and thick pancake-like batter.

NOTES:

- This was made a tad bland due to the heat in the filling it would go over. Add some heat or spices if desired. Curry powder, tumeric, cayenne pepper, hot sauce, prepared horseradish, additional wet mustard, and cumin powder, would all work well.

- Makes enough for two 12" to 14" pizzas (from 2 lbs. of dough).

Cauliflower, Millet, and Carrot Sauce

INGREDIENTS:

- 1 cups cauliflower (chopped, 1/2" pieces)
- 1/2 cup uncooked millet
- 1/3 cup raw carrot (diced)
- 2 cups water
- 1 t. garlic powder
- 1 t. salt (optional)
- 2 T. corn starch
- 2 T. wet mustard
- 1 t. red Tabasco sauce
- 1 cup water

METHOD:

1. Bring first 5 ingredients to a boil in a small pot, then simmer on lowest heat setting for 25 to 30 minutes. Turn off heat, and let sit covered for 10 minutes. Uncover and let cool to room temperature. If necessary, drain.

2. Put vegetable mixture into a blender or food processor (mash a little with

the back of a wooden spoon)

3. Add remaining ingredients, reserving the water to add in small increments, gradually increasing the processing speed until the mixture is a smooth and thick pancake-like batter.

VARIATIONS:

- Depending upon the type of pizza being made, fresh or dried herbs can be added and hand mixed into the batter when smooth.
- Mix in chopped canned green chiles and sliced black olives with leftover sauce to make nachos (pour over tortilla chips, etc., and heat) or in quesadillas.

NOTE:

- This recipes makes around 3 1/2 cups of sauce.

Potato, Carrot, and Ginger Sauce

INGREDIENTS:

- 1 cup peeled chopped potato
- 1/3 cup peeled chopped carrot
- 2 cloves garlic
- 1 t. ground ginger
- 1 t. ground cinnamon
- 2 T. corn starch
- 3/4 cup water + 1/4 cup Sherry (or water)

METHOD:

1. Cover potatoes and carrots with water in a small pot. Bring to a boil, cover, turn very low, and let simmer for a few minutes until "fork tender." Remove cover, let cool to room temperature.
2. Add the drained vegetables and remaining ingredients to a blender or food processor, and process until mixture is a smooth thick batter.

VARIATION:

- Add 1/4 cup of nuts when processing vegetable mixture.

NOTE:

- This recipe makes enough for two 12" to 14" pizzas.

Sweet Potato, Oats, Carrot, and Green Chili Sauce

INGREDIENTS:

- 1 cup raw sweet potato (peeled, 1/2" dice)
- 1/2 cup carrots (1/4" dice)
- 2/3 cup rolled oats
- 4 oz. can chopped, diced chilies (undrained)
- 1 T. Dijon mustard (to taste)
- 2 T. corn starch
- 1 to 1 1/4 cup water (water plus leftover cooking broth)

METHOD:

1. Cover potatoes and carrots with water in a small pot. Bring to a boil, and let simmer for a few minutes until "fork tender." Remove cover, let cool.
2. Add drained vegetables and remaining ingredients to a blender or food processor, reserving the water.
3. Add liquid in incremental amounts, blending carefully until a smooth pancake-like batter consistency has been achieved.

NOTE:

- This recipe makes more than enough sauce for two 12" to 14" pizzas (around 3 1/2 cups).

Chapter 4: Powerful Pizza Possibilities

"Without question, the greatest invention in the history of mankind is beer. Oh, I grant you that the wheel was also a fine invention, but the wheel does not go nearly as well with pizza."

--- Dave Barry

A truly Heart Healthy pizza is greater than the sum of it's parts. Seen as an architectural structure composed of a foundation and "plant-based scaffolding" it is a synergistic collective. Another perspective would liken a fine pizza to a well-trained symphony, where each vegetable, herb, or spice, is a harmonious player in a grand composition.

My personal preference is to think of a pizza as a three- dimensional canvas, and the person creating the pie is akin to an artist, envisioning flavor and texture dynamics, carefully selecting from their paint palette appropriate ingredients, and then arranging them on the pizza crust to their own unique taste and visual aesthetics. Some people prefer to pile on a lot of ingredients on one end of the fillings spectrum, while on the other end some take a more minimalist approach, where it is proclaimed "less is more."

With that range of layout possibilities in mind, this final chapter provides many suggested combinations of vegetables, crusts, and sauces for Heart Healthy pizza cooks to experiment with and decide for themselves the amounts, types, and placement patterns on their own canvas. Some recipes have measurements for layering ingredients, others are suggested with a broad brush, urging creativity in deciding how much to use and how best to arrange on said canvas.

After all, there is no correct pizza and the following suggestions should not be taken as the final word for any given approach. Ideally, they will inspire you to try new combinations of taste and texture, and relish the fun of discovering what works and what doesn't.

TIPS AND TECHNIQUES:

- Be sure to take into account the moisture (or water content) of your veggies when using a thin crust. If zucchini is cut too thick and used on a very thin crust, the pizza might get soggy.

- Sprinkle finely chopped cooked or raw tender greens onto the prepared and shaped dough, and add sliced, diced, crushed tomatoes. This will tenderize the greens during cooking.

- Finely chopped onions are interesting as they add a neat texture and more "moisture" to the pizza than if they are sliced. Same holds true for peppers. A gourmet approach is to gently saute thinly sliced onions in white or red wine until most of the wine has evaporated and the onions start to take on a brownish tint.

- Leftover prepped filling vegetables can be put to good use in wraps, soups, on top of salads, or as part of a stir-fry for pasta. Leftover sauces can be used in a similar fashion.

- Freeze leftover pizza in slices to re-heat at around 375 degrees F. for 20 minutes or thereabouts.

- Experiment with overlapping slices in rows, having some fun with alternating slices of color (like thinly sliced summer squashes), not just for the visual nature, but for a different texture profile when eaten.

- A favorite approach to laying out the filling ingredients is to leave enough space in between them so that glimmers of the bottom sauce or vegetables can still be seen when the pizza is completed. This also enables some of the topping sauce to seep down into these "crevasses," giving the pizza slices a "fuller" taste and texture feel.

OLD WORLD PIZZA CONCEPTS:

Pizza Margherita

CRUST:
- Basic Pizza Dough (p. 14)

LAYERING INGREDIENTS:
- Classic Tomato Sauce (p. 25, omit basil)
- fresh or dried basil
- "Millet, Sunflower Seeds, and Oregano Sauce" (p. 55, omit oregano)
- "Parmiso" (recipe follows)

METHOD:
1. Pre-heat oven to 425 or 450 degrees F. (depending upon your oven)
2. Pour and spread Classic Tomato Sauce on prepared dough.
3. Sprinkle basil on sauce.
4. Pour topping sauce on in clumps or blobs to resemble visual appearance and texture of mozzarella slices.
5. Sprinkle with Parmiso.

6. Bake pizza at 425 to 450 degrees F. for 15 to 20 minutes.

VARIATION:

- Instead of the tomato sauce, use slices of fresh tomatoes, and sprinkled the dried basil or chopped fresh basil on top of them.

Parmiso Recipe

INGREDIENTS:

- 3 T. roasted sesame seeds
- 1 T. flax seeds
- 2 T. nutritional yeast
- 1/4 to 1/2 t. salt (to taste)

METHOD:

1. If not using pre-roasted sesame seeds, roast sesame seeds in a dry skillet (optional).

2. Add all ingredients to a spice or coffee mill.

3. Grind vigorously until you have a fine powder.

VARIATIONS:

- Substitute any amount of either sesame or flax seeds with equal amount of ground blanched sliced almonds.
- Use less sesame seeds and more flax seeds as desired.
- Add 1/2 t. powdered sea vegetable (dulse, kombu, or nori).

NOTES:

- This recipe was created as a combination of a plant-based grated Parmesan Cheese and Gomiso. Gomiso is a ground roasted sesame seed and salt mixture, very popular in macrobiotic cooking as well as in Asia (particularly, Korea).
- This should be made in small amounts and not stored in the refrigerator, but instead, in a well-sealed glass jar or use a herb or container that no longer has the original herb or spice in it (making it easy to "sprinkle" on your pizzas, pastas, soups, and steamed vegetables).

Pizza Putanesca with Tempeh Anchovies

CRUST:

- Basic Pizza Dough (p. 14)

LAYERING INGREDIENTS:

- Classic Tomato Sauce (p. 25, use "puttanesca" variation and replace red wine with water)
- Tempeh Anchovies (recipe follows)
- White Beans and Millet Sauce (p. 75)
- sliced black and/or green olives

METHOD:

1. Pre-heat oven to 425 or 450 degrees F. (depending upon your oven)
2. Pour and spread Classic Tomato Sauce on prepared dough.
3. Arrange tempeh anchovies on top of sauce.
4. Pour topping sauce onto pizza.
5. Put olive slices on topping sauce.
6. Bake pizza for 15 to 20 minutes.

Tempeh Anchovies Recipe

INGREDIENTS:

- 1 piece of kombu (6" long)
- 1 8 oz. package of soy tempeh
- 1/3 cup red wine + 2/3 cup water (as necessary)
- 2 to 4 T. low-sodium Tamari, soy sauce, or Bragg's (see Glossary, p. 133)
- 1/2 cup grated or finely diced onion
- 3 to 4 T. lemon juice

METHOD:

1. Rinse the salt off the kombu.
2. Slice kombu crosswise into 1/4" to 1/2" slices.
3. Lay tempeh flat on a cutting board, and slice into finger-sized strips around 1/4" x 1.2" thick.
4. Combine kombu, tempeh, wine, water (to just covering tempeh slices),

and Tamari in a sauce pan or pot, bring to a boil, cover. Lower heat and simmer 5 minutes. Let cool.

5. Put mixture into a rectangular glass dish large enough so that the slices all lay flat.

6. Add remaining ingredients, and gently shaking the dish back and forth to make sure the marinade covers tempeh completely.

7. Cover, let marinate for a least an hour, or better, overnight.

8. Optional: lightly fry tempeh slices on both sides in a non-stick pan, or bake the slices on a non-stick cookie sheet at 350 degrees F. until crisp (15 to 25 minutes).

VARIATION:

• Other types of sea vegetables (nori, arame, dulse, etc.) can also be used in place of kombu.

NOTE:

• Leftover marinade can be thickened with corn starch to make a salad dress, while kombu strips can be added to soups, sauces, or stews.

Pizza Genovese

CRUST:

• Basic Pizza Dough (p. 14)

LAYERING INGREDIENTS:

• Basil Pesto (p. 30)
• 1 potato (Yukon preferred)
• garlic powder (optional, to taste)
• ground pepper (optional, to taste)
• 1/2 to 1 red onion (sliced or diced fine)
• Parmiso (p. 90)

METHOD:

1. Pre-heat oven to 425 or 450 degrees F. (depending upon your oven)
2. Sliced unpeeled potato very thin (no more than 1/4" thick).
3. Bring water to boil in a small pot, and par-boil the slices around 1 minute.

They should still be firm, but not break up when gently poked with a sharp knife or fork.

4. Drain, and let cool. Gently pat dry with a towel (paper or dish).
5. Smooth Basil Pesto on shaped pizza dough.
6. Gently arrange potato slices on pesto (overlapping if desired) and press them down slightly into the pesto.
7. Sprinkle with garlic powder and ground pepper.
8. Add red onions.
9. Sprinkle with Parmiso
10. Bake pizza for 15 to 20 minutes.

NOTES:

- If using a mandoline to slice potatoes very thin, there will be no need to pre-cook the potatoes.
- The amount of potatoes to use varies with how much they are overlapped on the pizza and how large a pizza being made. Generally, 1 to 2 medium potatoes per 12 to 14" pizza.
- Raw potato slices can also be pre-cooked on a no-stick baking sheet at 375 degrees F. until the edges start to turn brown (15 to 20 minutes).

Pizza Florentine

CRUST:

- Basic Pizza Dough (p. 14)

LAYERING INGREDIENTS:

- chopped fresh spinach
- tomatoes (sliced, or sauce of choice)
- fresh or dried rosemary (to taste)
- artichoke hearts (15 oz. packed in water, about 1 1/2 cups quartered)
- Oats, Cannellini Beans, and Garlic Sauce (p. 58)
- Parmiso (optional, p. 90)

METHOD:

1. Pre-heat oven to 425 or 450 degrees F. (depending upon your oven)
2. Sprinkle chopped spinach on prepared dough.

3. Arrange tomato slices on spinach.

4. Sprinkle tomato slices with rosemary.

5. Drain artichoke hearts, slice crosswise into 1 to 1.25" pieces.

6. Arrange artichoke heart pieces on top of tomatoes.

7. Pour on topping sauce.

8. Sprinkle on Parmiso.

9. Bake pizza for 15 to 20 minutes.

Pizza Fungi

CRUST:

- Basic Pizza Dough (p. 14)

LAYERING INGREDIENTS:

- red chili pepper flakes (optional)
- tomatoes (sliced, or sauce of choice)
- garlic powder
- Gimme Lean Sausage (or TVP sausage, recipe below)
- ground pepper (to taste)
- mushrooms (sliced, a mixture, or type of choice)
- Sherry (or preferred liquid)
- dried thyme
- low-salt Tamari (or soy sauce)
- Barley and Almonds Sauce (p. 46)

METHOD:

1. Pre-heat oven to 425 or 450 degrees F. (depending upon your oven)

2. Sprinkle red chili pepper flakes on prepared and shaped dough.

3. Layer dough with tomato slices.

4. Sprinkle garlic powder on the tomatoes.

5. Pinch off pieces of Gimme Lean sausage and place on tomatoes sparingly (alternately, sprinkle with TVP sausage).

6. Sprinkle ground pepper on the pizza.

7. Saute sliced mushrooms with Sherry (or liquid of choice), some dried thyme, and a little Tamari until they start to soften. Turn off heat, let cool, drain.

8. Assemble mushrooms on pizza.

9. Pour on topping sauce.

10. Bake pizza for 15 to 20 minutes.

VARIATIONS:

- Sprinkle drained sliced black olives on top of pizza.

NOTE:

- Instead of purchasing "cooking sherry" in a grocery store, pick up an inexpensive Sherry at a liquor store and enjoy the higher quality at a lesser cost.

TVP Sausage Recipe

INGREDIENTS:

- 1 cup TVP unflavored granules (see Glossary (p.143))
- 1 cup of water
- 1 T. low salt Tamari or soy sauce
- 1 - 2 T. red wine vinegar
- 1/2 t. liquid smoke (optional)
- 1 t. red chili pepper flakes
- 1/2 t. onion powder
- 1 t. garlic powder
- 1 t. ground sage
- 1 t. ground thyme
- 1/2 t. paprika
- 1/2 t. fennel seeds (ground in spice mill)
- several drops of red Tabasco sauce (to taste)
- 1/2 t. black pepper (to taste)

METHOD:

1. Mix together all ingredients except for the TVP granules in a small pot. Bring to a boil, then turn heat on low.

2. Add TVP granules and stir. Cover pot and turn off heat.

3. Wait 15 minutes, uncover, and stir with spoon or fork to "fluff" the mixture. If need be, drain TVP.

4. TVP can now be used as is, or lightly browned in a non-stick frying pan.

VARIATION:
- Substitute TVP cubes for granules.

METHOD:
1. Put all ingredients into a pot and mix. Use enough water to cover the cubes about 1/2". Bring to a boil, cover, turn heat down very low to simmer for 10 minutes.
2. Turn off heat, let sit for 5 minutes. Drain, and let cool.
3. Cubes can be used as is, or lightly browned in a non-stick frying pan.

Pizza Norma

CRUST:
- Basic Pizza Dough (p. 14)

LAYERING INGREDIENTS:
- Rice and Sunflower Seeds Sauce (p. 69)
- eggplant (sliced thin, crosswise)
- Classic Tomato Sauce (p. 25)
- Parmiso (p. 90)

METHOD:
1. Pre-heat oven to 425 or 450 degrees F. (depending upon your oven)
2. Pour and smooth topping sauce on prepared and shaped dough.
3. Place eggplant slices on a non-stick cookie sheet and broil in oven until they just start to turn color (brownish). Take out, let cool to room temperature.
4. Arrange eggplant slices on pizza.
5. Top with tomato sauce.
6. Sprinkle with Parmiso.
7. Bake pizza for 15 to 20 minutes.

VARIATIONS:
- Sprinkle chopped fresh herbs on top of eggplant after adding tomato sauce.

- Substitute Tofu Ricotta (p. 34) for the Rice and Sunflower Seeds Sauce.

Pizza Caponata

CRUST:
- Basic Pizza Dough (p. 14)

LAYERING INGREDIENTS:
- Classic Tomato Sauce (p. 25)
- capers (optional)
- 1/2 to 1 eggplant (sliced thin, crosswise)
- balsamic or red wine vinegar
- nutritional yeast
- dried red chili pepper flakes
- 1 red or green pepper (seeded, cut in thin circular slices)
- 1 stick celery (cut crosswise into thin slices)
- 1 onion (cut in thin circular slices)
- sliced olives (green and/or black)
- Millet, Sunflower Seeds, and Oregano Sauce (p. 55)

METHOD:
1. Pre-heat oven to 425 or 450 degrees F. (depending upon your oven)
2. Pour and smooth tomato sauce on prepared and shaped dough.
3. Sprinkle drained capers lightly onto sauce.
4. Place eggplant slices on a non-stick cookie sheet and broil in oven until they just start to turn color (brownish). Take out, let cool.
5. Arrange eggplant slices on pizza.
6. Lightly brush some vinegar on the slices.
7. Sprinkle eggplant with nutritional yeast.
8. Arrange pepper slices on top of eggplant.
9. Sprinkle diced celery onto pizza.
10. Arrange onion slices.
11. Sprinkle sliced olives on top.
12. Pour on topping sauce.
13. Bake pizza for 15 to 20 minutes.

- Substitute sliced tomatoes for the Classic Tomato Sauce, and sprinkle them with chopped fresh or dried basil and/or marjoram as well as some garlic powder.

Pizza Corn Polenta

CRUST:

- Corn Polenta (p. 17)

LAYERING INGREDIENTS:

- Navy Beans, Rice, and Fresh Basil Sauce (p. 73)
- thinly sliced tomatoes
- dried red chili pepper flakes (optional)
- garlic powder
- thinly sliced onions
- Parmiso (p. 90)

METHOD:

1. Pre-heat oven to 425 or 450 degrees F. (depending upon your oven)
2. Pour and smooth (if necessary) sauce onto prepared and shaped pizza dough.
3. Arrange sliced tomatoes on top of sauce.
4. Sprinkle tomatoes with red chili pepper flakes and garlic powder.
5. Arrange a layer of onions.
6. Sprinkle liberally with Parmiso.
7. Bake pizza until onions and tomatoes start to brown.

VARIATIONS:

- Substitute garlic powder with finely chopped garlic
- Add chopped raw spinach or swiss chard (minus ribs) before laying down the tomatoes.

NEW WORLD PIZZA CONCEPTS:

Nearly Nouveaux Mex

CRUST:

- Whole Wheat Dough (p. 15)

LAYERING INGREDIENTS:

- Corn Comfort Sauce (p. 36)
- 1 15 oz. can pinto beans
- chili powder
- 1 green pepper (medium to large)
- 1 onion (white or red)
- 2 jalapenos
- Millet, Cashews, and Mustard Sauce (p. 53)

METHOD:

1. Pre-heat oven to 425 or 450 degrees F. (depending upon your oven).
2. Rinse and drain pinto beans.
3. Clean and slice green pepper, onion, and jalapenos (removing membranes and seeds).
4. (optional) Broil sliced vegetables on a non-stick cookie sheet until starting to brown and blister. Let cool.
5. Pour corn sauce on prepared and shaped dough.
6. Add desired amount of pinto beans.
7. Sprinkle pinto beans with chili powder.
8. Arrange vegetables on pizza.
9. Pour on the topping sauce.
10. Bake pizza for 15 to 20 minutes.

Southwestern Special

CRUST:

- Basic Pizza Dough (p. 14, substituting 1 cup of flour with 1 cup semolina flour)

LAYERING INGREDIENTS:

- 1 cup raw spinach (chopped)
- sliced tomatoes
- 1 cup cooked pinto beans (rinsed and drained)
- chili powder
- 1 small onion (thinly sliced)
- fresh coriander (optional, chopped)
- 1/2 cup corn
- sliced black olives
- red Tabasco sauce (optional)
- Quinoa, Artichoke Hearts, and Sunflower Seeds Sauce (p. 62) or Millet, Avocado, and Oregano Sauce (p. 51)
- ground black pepper or paprika

METHOD:

1. Pre-heat oven to 425 or 450 degrees F. (depending upon your oven)
2. Sprinkle spinach onto prepared and shaped dough.
3. Arrange tomato slices on top of spinach.
4. Sprinkle the pinto beans on top of the tomatoes.
5. Sprinkle lightly with chili powder.
6. Layer the onions.
7. Sprinkle on the coriander.
8. Sprinkle the corn onto the pizza.
9. Arrange olives on top.
10. Put drops of Tabasco sauce on (to taste).
11. Pour on the topping sauce.
12. Sprinkle with ground pepper or paprika.
13. Bake pizza for 15 to 20 minutes.

VARIATIONS:

- For a spicy southwestern "kick" add in 1/2 to 1 T. cayenne pepper when the pizza dough is being kneaded.

The Official Mad Cowboy

CRUST:

- Whole Wheat Crust (p. 15)

LAYERING INGREDIENTS:

- crushed tomatoes
- fresh chopped or dried rosemary
- red onions (chopped)
- fresh shiitake mushrooms (sliced)
- red peppers (sliced)
- eggplant (thinly sliced in small strips)
- caraway seeds
- pineapple chunks (drained)
- broccoli flowerettes
- Oats, Pinto Beans, and Salsa Sauce (p. 60)
- sauerkraut (drained, rinsed with water, drained)

METHOD:

1. Pre-heat oven to 425 or 450 degrees F. (depending upon your oven).
2. Layer all ingredients, in order, on the prepared and shaped dough, being careful to leave sufficient space between ingredients for others.
3. Bake pizza for 15 to 20 minutes.

NOTE:

- Howard Lyman,"The Mad Cowboy," indicated exactly what he wanted on this pizza and in what order as it was being created. Today, the "Oats, Pinto Beans, and Salsa Sauce" (Page. 60) is the one he'd undoubtedly enjoy.

Thymely Summer Squash

CRUST:

- 1 lb. pizza dough of choice

LAYERING INGREDIENTS:

- thinly sliced tomatoes

- red chili pepper flakes
- Oats, Carrot, Corn Sauce (p. 59)
- 2 heaping T. finely chopped fresh thyme (de-stemmed)
- sliced summer squash (very thin circles, yellow and green)
- garlic powder to taste
- freshly ground black pepper to taste

METHOD:
1. Pre-heat oven to 425 or 450 degrees F. (depending upon your oven).
2. Layer ingredients in order indicated.
3. Bake pizza for 15 to 20 minutes.

VARIATIONS:
- Sprinkle finely chopped mushrooms on the squash slices, then sprinkle with ground black pepper.

NOTE:
- Be sure to lightly press the sliced squash into the bottom sauce.

Friendly Frankfurters & Kale

CRUST:
- Whole Wheat Dough (p. 15)

LAYERING INGREDIENTS:
- tender raw kale leaves (rinsed, drained, de-stemmed and chopped)
- sliced tomatoes
- sliced onions
- sliced no-fat tofu hot dogs sliced crosswise (see Glossary)
- sweet pickle relish (optional)
- mustard of choice (use a squeeze bottle to apply)
- Chickpea, Oats, and Pimentos Sauce (p. 72)

METHOD:
1. Pre-heat oven to 425 or 450 degrees F. (depending upon your oven).
2. Make a 1/4" layer of kale on top of prepared and shaped dough.

3. Arrange tomato slices.

4. Put on onion slices.

5. Sprinkle with hot dog slices.

6. Dot with pickle relish

7. Apply mustard.

8. Pour on topping sauce.

9. Bake pizza for 15 to 20 minutes.

VARIATIONS:

- Substitute left-over or canned chili for mustard and/or relish.
- Substitute drained, rinsed, then drained again, sauerkraut to relish and mustard (as desired).

Artsy Artichoke, Mushroom, and Corn

CRUST:

- 1 lb. pizza dough of choice

LAYERING INGREDIENTS:

- 1 cup finely diced mushrooms
- 1 14 oz. can water-packed artichoke hearts (drained, quartered)
- 1 cup roasted corn kernels
- sliced black olives
- Lima Beans, Millet, and Flax Seed Sauce (p. 72)
- ground black pepper

METHOD:

1. Pre-heat oven to 425 or 450 degrees F. (depending upon your oven).

2. Sprinkle on mushrooms.

3. Add artichokes and press gently into sauce (leave some room between the artichokes).

4. Sprinkle on corn.

5. Add sliced olives.

6. Pour on topping sauce.

7. Sprinkle with black pepper.

8. Bake pizza for 15 to 20 minutes.

Sausage, Broccoli, and Mushrooms

CRUST:

- prepared pizza dough of choice

LAYERING INGREDIENTS:

- crushed canned tomatoes
- broccoli flowerets
- Gimme Lean Sausage (or TVP Sausage, p. 95)
- mushrooms (sliced)
- onions (sliced)
- capers (optional)
- Millet, Sprouted Sunflower Seeds and Dijon Mustard Sauce (p. 56)
- paprika

METHOD:

1. Pre-heat oven to 425 or 450 degrees F. (depending upon your oven).
2. If using, saute Gimme Lean Sausage (recipe below).
3. Add ingredients to pizza dough in the order indicated.
4. Bake pizza for 15 to 20 minutes.

Sauteed Gimme Lean Sausage Recipe

1. Add desired amount of sausage to a non-stick skillet.
2. Add some red wine (or liquid of choice), low-salt Tamari, dried or fresh chopped thyme (optional), and ground pepper to taste.
3. Bring skillet to low to medium heat, frequently breaking up the sausage using a wooden or plastic spoon.
4. Stir-fry until sausage starts to turn brown, adding more liquid of choice if need be to keep sausage from sticking.

Over the Rainbow Chard

CRUST:

- Basic Pizza Dough (p. 14)

LAYERING INGREDIENTS:

- tomatoes (crushed)
- sausage-flavored TVP granules (optional, see "TVP Sausage" recipe on p. 95)
- rainbow swiss chard stir-fried ("Stir-Fried Greens" recipe follows)
- fresh or dried herb of choice (optional)
- raisins (optional)
- Barley, White Beans, and Horseradish Sauce (p. 47)
- ground pepper (optional)

METHOD:

1. Pre-heat oven to 425 or 450 degrees F. (depending upon your oven).
2. Arrange tomatoes on prepared and shaped pizza dough.
3. Sprinkle TVP granules onto tomatoes.
4. Spoon drained stir-fried greens onto tomatoes.
5. Sprinkle herb(s) of choice onto greens.
6. Sprinkle raisins on top of greens
7. Pour topping sauce on pizza.
8. Sprinkle with ground pepper.
9. Bake pizza for 15 to 20 minutes.

VARIATIONS:

- Toasted (or raw) unsalted nuts can also be sprinkled on top of the chard on the pizza, pine nuts being a favorite (although expensive and a bit high in fat).

Stir-fried Greens Recipe

INGREDIENTS:

- 1/3 cup red wine (or liquid of choice)
- red chili pepper flakes (optional)
- garlic powder (or fresh minced garlic)
- 1 lb. swiss chard (rainbow, or green)
- low-sodium Tamari (or soy sauce)
- balsamic vinegar (or vinegar of choice)

METHOD:

1. Add first three ingredients to a non-stick wok or large stir-fry pan.

2. Separate ribs from leaves of chard by carefully running a knife down both sides of the rib. Slice ribs into small pieces (treat them like celery) and put into a salad spinner. Add water, drain, and spin them a few times (they don't have to be completely dry).

3. Put sliced ribs into wok.

4. Coarsely cut chard leaves so that they will fit, in batches if need be, into salad spinner. Fill with water, drain, and spin.

5. Cut chard into slices, or coarsely chop (depending upon personal preference). Add cut chard to wok. Cover, and bring to medium heat. Check after about 5 minutes and see if the liquid is starting to simmer, turning heat higher if need be. The goal is to get the liquid to a simmer to first cook the ribs, and then to gradually soften the leaves.

6. Check every few minutes, adding more water if need be.

7. After around 15 minutes (depending upon heat level), sprinkle some vinegar and tamari around the top of the chard leaves.

8. Taking a large wooden or plastic spoon, start mixing the leaves with the ribs. The leaves will start to increasingly wilt.

9. Turn heat low, and keep covered, periodically checking liquid level. When the leaves are pretty much all cooked, stir them again, and move to the outside part of the wok. If there's liquid left over, you can either let them steam a bit longer cover, or remove with a slotted spoon.

VARIATIONS:

- Greens can be mixed. Spinach, chard, mustard greens, and dandelion greens are good choices for combining. Remember that greens really cook down. A full wok of greens will cook down to about 2 to 3 servings!

Terrific Tri-Pepper

CRUST:

- pizza dough of choice

LAYERING INGREDIENTS:

- tomato (sliced)

- orange, yellow, and red sweet peppers (thinly sliced)
- dried oregano (optional)
- onions (sliced)
- pimento-stuffed green olives (sliced)
- Quinoa, Artichoke Hearts, and Dijon Mustard Sauce (p. 61)

METHOD:

1. Pre-heat oven to 425 or 450 degrees F. (depending upon your oven)
2. Arrange tomato slices on top of prepared and shaped dough.
3. Arrange pepper slices on top of tomatoes.
4. Sprinkle pizza with dried oregano.
5. Arrange onion slices on top of the pizza.
6. Sprinkle on the sliced green olives.
7. Pour on the topping sauce.
8. Bake pizza for 15 to 20 minutes.

NOTES:

- Frozen sliced peppers can also be used. Let thaw out, drain, and dab them dry with paper towels or a dish towel. Can be used as is, or sauteed lightly in white wine or white Vermouth.

Jumbo Gingered Gumbo

CRUST:

- Basic Pizza Dough (p. 14, substituting one cup of flour with cornmeal)

LAYERING INGREDIENTS:

- red chili pepper flakes
- thinly sliced tomatoes
- garlic powder
- chili powder
- eggplant (sliced thin, crosswise)
- fresh or dried thyme
- okra (cut in 1/4" rounds)
- sliced green pepper

- sliced onion
- fresh or dried oregano
- garlic (minced) or garlic power
- red Tabasco sauce (optional)
- Millet, Black-eyed Peas, and Ginger Sauce (p. 52)
- paprika

METHOD:

1. Pre-heat oven to 425 or 450 degrees F. (depending upon your oven)
2. Slice eggplant into strips.
3. Broil eggplant and okra slices on a non-stick cooking sheet or lightly oiled baking dish until they start to turn color.
4. Sprinkle red chili pepper flakes on prepared and shaped dough.
5. Arrange tomato slices on dough.
6. Sprinkle tomatoes with garlic and chili powder.
7. Arrange eggplant to slightly overlap tomatoes.
8. Sprinkle eggplant with thyme.
9. Add okra, green peppers, and onions.
10. Sprinkle with oregano.
11. Dot the pizza top with drops of Tabasco sauce (to taste).
12. Pour on topping sauce.
13. Sprinkle with paprika.
14. Bake pizza for 15 to 20 minutes.

VARIATIONS:

- Roasting/broiling the tomato slices until they start to turn brown will add a nice 'charred' taste to the pizza filling.
- Sprinkle a little balsamic vinegar on the eggplant before sprinkling on the thyme.

NOTE:

- If you can find it, use pre-roasted cornmeal in making the dough. It adds nice "body" to the pizza crust.

Really Reubenesque

CRUST:

- Pumpernickel or Rye Dough (p. 15)

LAYERING INGREDIENTS:

- 3 cups cabbage (chopped or sliced thin)
- 1 cup (or more) mushrooms (sliced)
- paprika (optional)
- 1 sliced onion
- Thousand Island Dressing Sauce (p. 30)
- Mark's Mashed-Up Potatoes Sauce(p. 36)
- ground pepper (optional)

METHOD:

1. Arrange cabbage on prepared and shaped dough.
2. Top the cabbage with sliced mushrooms and and sprinkle both with paprika.
3. Arrange onion slices on top of the vegetables.
4. Pour and spread the first topping sauce.
5. Gently spread the 2nd topping sauce on top of the other.
6. Sprinkle with ground pepper.

VARIATIONS:

- The Thousand Island Dressing Sauce can also be put on the pizza first, followed by vegetables, et. al.
- Saute mushrooms and onions lightly in cooking sherry or beer, and drain, before putting on pizza.

Powerful Pepperoni and Mushroom

CRUST:

- Basic Pizza Dough (p. 14, substituting 1 cup of flour with semolina flour).

LAYERING INGREDIENTS:

- crushed or chopped and drained canned tomatoes

- Yves Vegan Cuisine Pepperoni (or plant-based pepperoni of choice)
- sliced mushrooms
- sliced green peppers
- sliced onions
- fresh or dry oregano
- minced garlic (optional)
- Rice, Oats, and Cashews Sauce (p. 68)
- sliced black olives

METHOD:

1. Pre-heat oven to 425 or 450 degrees F. (depending upon your oven).
2. Arrange tomatoes on prepared and shaped dough.
3. Place pepperoni slices on pizza, leaving enough room between slices to see tomato "area" between slices about the same size as the slices.
4. Arrange mushroom slices on pizza.
5. Add green peppers and onions.
6. Sprinkle pizza with oregano.
7. Pour on topping sauces
8. Arrange black olive slices on top of sauce.
9. Bake pizza for 15 to 20 minutes.

VARIATIONS:

- Substitute Yves pepperoni with Yves Canadian Bacon, sliced in fourths or halved.

Roasty Veggielicious

CRUST:

- Basic Pizza Dough (p. 14)

LAYERING INGREDIENTS:

- 2 medium tomatoes
- 1 zucchini or yellow squash
- 1 sweet red or green pepper
- 1 1/2 cups broccoli flowerets
- 1 red onion

- whole mushrooms
- dried herb(s) of choice
- low-sodium Tamari, soy sauce, or salt (optional)
- balsamic vinegar (optional)
- ground pepper (optional)
- topping sauce of choice

METHOD:
1. Prepare and roast the vegetables (recipe follows).
2. Assemble roasted vegetables onto the topping sauce.
3. Pour on topping sauce.
4. Bake pizza at for 15 to 20 minutes.

Roasting Vegetables Method

1. Pre-heat oven to 425 degrees F.
2. Very lightly oil a heat-proof casserole dish or non-stick baking pan.
3. Cut vegetables into 1 inch pieces. Keep mushrooms whole unless very large, then cut in half. The onion should be cut in thick "crescents" of like size as the vegetables.
4. Spread vegetables onto pan. If there's not enough room to put all the vegetables in one layer, then put the denser ones on bottom first.
5. Sprinkle low-salt tamari judiciously over vegetables (or, sprinkle with a small amount of salt).
6. Sprinkle vegetables with balsamic vinegar (optional), then herbs and ground pepper.
7. Bake in oven, uncovered, for about 15 minutes (this will vary depending upon how your oven is calibrated). The vegetables should be starting to brown and carmelize. Mix them a bit with a large wooden or plastic spoon, or, being careful with an oven mitt, shake the pan a few times to re-distribute the vegetables a bit.
8. Bake until they start to get dark brown (another 15 minutes).
9. Remove from oven, let cool to room temperature.

NOTE:

- Just about any vegetable can be roasted, and the roasting process can really bring out their flavor. Try eggplant, fennel, cauliflower, and even brussels sprouts (halved).

OTHER WORLD RECIPES:

Gratefully Greek

CRUST:

- Basic Pizza Dough (p. 14)

LAYERING INGREDIENTS:

- sliced tomatoes
- fresh or dried oregano
- artichokes (drained and quartered)
- Tofu Feta Cheese (cubes or crumbled, recipe follows)
- thinly sliced red onions
- sliced black olives
- ground black pepper (optional)

METHOD:

1. Pre-heat oven to 425 or 450 degrees F. (depending upon your oven).
2. Arrange tomatoes on prepared and shaped dough.
3. Sprinkle with oregano.
4. Add artichokes and Tofu Feta Cheese.
5. Layer on onions and black olives.
6. Sprinkle with black pepper.
7. Bake pizza for 15 to 20 minutes.

VARIATIONS:

- Add sliced antipasta-style pickled hot peppers.
- Sprinkle pizza with nutritional yeast or Parmiso (p. 90).

Tofu Feta Cheese Recipe

INGREDIENTS:

- 1/2 lb. firm or extra-firm tofu (not Mori-Nu)
- 1 cup water
- 1/4 cup red wine vinegar
- 1 t. salt (optional) or 1 T. low-sodium Tamari or Soy Sauce (to taste)
- 1 t. garlic powder
- 1/4 t. ground black pepper (to taste)

METHOD:

1. Rinse tofu block, and carefully slice lengthwise into 4 equal width pieces.
2. Place the slices side-by-side on 3 or 4 paper towels on the counter, and carefully wrap them so there's a couple of layers of towel on both sides.
3. Carefully wrap toweled-tofu with a cloth towel, again, the tofu slices should still be flat side down.
4. Place cutting board on top of the wrapped tofu, and put a heavy weight on top (one that won't easily tip over). A gallon jug of water works well.
5. Let sit for 30 minutes or thereabouts, letting the water be pressed out of the tofu.
6. Unwrap tofu and cut into 1/2" cubes (they don't have to be perfect cubes!).
7. Whisk water, vinegar, salt, garlic powder, and pepper in a bowl.
8. Layer tofu in a glass or plastic container, gently shaking the container to move some of the marinade on all parts of the tofu.
9. Cover, and let sit in a refrigerator overnight (or longer), occasionally mixing the marinade and tofu, shaking the container, or turning the cubes over.

VARIATION:

- Boil, cover, and simmer a 6" strip of kombu cut in 1/2" pieces in two cups of water for about 20 minutes. Let cool to room temperature. Use 3/4 of the remaining broth instead of plain water to marinate the tofu.
- Add 2 1/2 T. of nutritional yeast to the marinade.
- Add 1 T. of dried basil to the marinade.

NOTES:

- Makes enough Tofu Feta Cheese for 1 1b. pizza (12" to 14").

- Tip: save leftover kombu pieces for soups, sauces or stews.

Spanakopizza

CRUST:

- Whole Wheat Dough (p. 15)

LAYERING INGREDIENTS:

- chopped raw spinach
- diced raw mushrooms
- fresh or dry thyme
- thinly sliced red onions
- Tofu Feta Cheese (p. 113, crumbled)
- black or green olives (sliced)

METHOD:

1. Pre-heat oven to 425 or 450 degrees F. (depending upon your oven).
2. Arrange spinach as a layer on top of prepared and shaped dough (at least 1/4 inch in height).
3. Put the mushrooms on top of the spinach as a full layer (1/4" in height).
4. Sprinkle thyme on top of the mushrooms.
5. Arrange the red onion slices on top of the mushrooms.
6. Sprinkle the Tofu Feta Cheese on top as densely as desired.
7. Sprinkle olives onto Tofu Feta Cheese, gently pressing them a bit.
8. Bake pizza for 15 to 20 minutes.

VARIATION:

- Sprinkle some nutritional yeast on top of the olives.

NOTE:

- Many thanks to the amazing and most prolific plant-based cookbook author on Earth, Robin Robertson, for dreaming up the name of this pizza in our early discussions about this book!

Krazy Kim Chi Please

CRUST:

- Whole Grain Rice Crust (p. 19)

LAYERING INGREDIENTS:

- Kim Chi (see Glossary (p. 137))
- sliced shiitake mushrooms (fresh or re-hydrated, see "Glossary")
- White Beans and Millet Sauce (p.75)
- sesame seeds (optional)

METHOD:

1. Pre-heat oven to 425 or 450 degrees F. (depending upon your oven).
2. Drain Kim Chi for several minutes, and if homemade, save the leftover liquid in a lidded jar in the refrigerator as a quick starter for the next batch.
3. Make a layer of Kim Chi on top of prepared and shaped dough.
4. Arrange mushrooms on top of the Kim Chi.
5. Pour topping sauce on pizza.
6. Sprinkle pizza with sesame seeds.
7. Bake pizza for 15 to 20 minutes.

Pleasing Polynesian

CRUST:

- Millet Polenta (p. 18)

LAYERING INGREDIENTS:

- tofu cubes
- cherry tomatoes (sliced in half)
- pineapple cubes
- mushrooms (sliced)
- green peppers (sliced in rings)
- Polynesian Sauce (p. 34)
- shredded non-sugared coconut (optional)

METHOD:

1. Pre-heat oven to 425 or 450 degrees F. (depending upon your oven).

2. Scatter arrange first three ingredients as a single layer on the Millet Polenta, leaving a little room between each ingredient for the topping sauce to flow through to the bottom.
3. Arrange the mushrooms and green peppers on top.
4. Pour on the topping sauce.
5. Sprinkle with coconut.
6. Bake pizza for 10 to 15 minutes.

VARIATION:
- Use snow peas (cut in half cross-wise) in place of tofu.

St. Patty's Pizza Pie

CRUST:
- Whole Wheat Dough (p. 15, adding 1 T. dried dill before mixing)

LAYERING INGREDIENTS:
- 1/2 cup carrots (sliced small julienne)
- 1/2 cup turnips (sliced small julienne)
- 1/2 cup parsnips (sliced small julienne)
- 1 cup diced cabbage
- 2 t. horseradish
- 1 t. wet mustard
- 1 t. dried parsley
- 1/4 cup white wine (or water)
- 1 t. soy sauce
- TVP Corned Beef Cubes (recipes follows)
- Barley, White Beans, and Horseradish Sauce (p. 47)
- 1 onion (sliced thin)
- paprika (optional)

METHOD:
1. Pre-heat oven to 425 or 450 degrees F. (depending upon your oven).
2. Put ingredients up to soy sauce into a non-stick (preferably) saute pan or wok. Bring to a slow boil, stirring to mix, and simmer on very low until most of the liquid is gone and the vegetables are still tender crisp. Drain, let cool

to room temperature.

3. Arrange vegetable mixture on prepared and shaped dough.

4. Sprinkle on TVP Corned Beef Cubes.

5. Arrange onion slices on top of pizza.

6. Pour topping sauce on pizza.

7. Sprinkle on paprika (to taste).

8. Bake pizza for 15 to 20 minutes.

VARIATION:

- Use 3/4 cup carrots and 3/4 cup cubed potatoes instead of 1/2 cup carrots, turnips, and parsnips. Be careful not to overcook the potatoes or they will be mushy.

TVP Corned Beef Cubes Recipe

INGREDIENTS:

- 1 cup unflavored TVP cubes
- 1/4 cup red wine vinegar
- 1/4 t. ground pepper (or to taste)
- 1 T. Ketchup
- 3/4 cup water
- 1 T. red Tabasco sauce

METHOD:

1. Put all ingredients into a small pot, mix, and slowly bring to a boil.

2. Simmer on very low for 10 to 15 minutes, turn off the heat, and let cool. Drain if necessary.

VARIATION:

- Substitute TVP cubes with tempeh cubes, reducing simmering time to 5 minutes.

Indian Samosa-Styled Pizza

CRUST:
- Basic Pizza Dough (p. 14, add 1 T. ground cumin during mixing)

LAYERING INGREDIENTS:
- Indian Spice White Sauce (p. 35)
- 1/4 cup water
- 1 T. mustard seeds (golden or dark)
- 1/4 t. salt
- 1/2 t. red pepper flakes
- 1/2 cup onions (sliced in half moons)
- 1 1/2 cup cabbage (chopped or thinly sliced)
- 1/4 t. garlic powder
- 1/2 cup shredded carrots
- 1 T. ground coriander
- 1/2 cup frozen peas (thawed, rinsed, drained)
- extra water as needed
- Mark's Mashed-Up Potatoes Sauce (p. 36, use Indian Variation)
- ground black pepper (optional)

METHOD:
1. Pre-heat oven to 425 or 450 degrees F. (depending upon your oven).
2. Put the water, mustard seeds, salt, and red chili pepper flakes into a wok or non-stick frying pan. Bring to a slow simmer and stir-fry a few minutes until the mustard seeds start to change color.
3. Add remaining vegetables and spices, stirring to mix. Cover, and on medium heat, continue stirring periodically until mixture is crisp tender. Add more water if necessary to keep vegetables from sticking.
4. Let cool, drain if necessary.
5. Spread or pour Indian Spice White Sauce on shaped dough.
6. Add stir-fried vegetables.
7. Smooth mashed potatoes on pizza.
8. Sprinkle on ground pepper.
9. Bake pizza for 15 to 20 minutes. Broiling a bit at the end of cooking will nicely brown the potato topping.

VARIATIONS:

- Sprinkle fresh chopped coriander or parsley on the pizza before adding the potatoes sauce.

Clever Curry

CRUST:

- Wheat and Millet Dough (p. 16)

LAYERING INGREDIENTS:
- water (or white wine, broth)
- cumin (seeds or powder, to taste)
- sliced onion
- sliced carrots
- fresh green beans (cut in 1 1/2" segments)
- sliced zucchini
- diced eggplant (peeling, optional)
- raisins
- sliced tomato
- curry powder (to taste)
- Indian Spice White Sauce (p. 35)
- shredded coconut (unsweetened, optional)

METHOD:
1. Pre-heat oven to 425 or 450 degrees F. (depending upon your oven).
2. Saute cumin, onions, and carrots for a few minutes in water (or white wine).
3. Add carrots, green beans, zucchini, eggplant, and curry powder. Continue stir-frying (adding more liquid if necessary) until the vegetables are crisp tender. Let cool to room temperature.
4. Arrange sliced tomatoes on prepared and shaped pizza dough. Sprinkle with curry powder.
5. Using a slotted spoon, put stir-fry mixture evenly onto tomatoes.
6. Pour on or spread Indian Spice White Sauce over the vegetables.
7. Sprinkle the top with the shredded coconut.
8. Bake pizza for 15 to 20 minutes.

VARIATIONS:
- All kinds of vegetables can be used in this basic recipe. If choosing to use a non-tofu-based topping sauce without legumes, then add some chickpeas to the stir-fry.
- Chopped nuts can also be added to the stir-fry, depending upon what topping sauce is chosen.

Vivid Vegetable Tarragon

CRUST:
- Basic Pizza Dough (p. 14)

LAYERING INGREDIENTS:
- 1 carrot (sliced)
- 1 cup cauliflower flowerets
- 1/2 onion (sliced)
- 1/2 green pepper (sliced)
- 2 T. white wine vinegar
- 1 T. of sugar (optional)
- 1 t. dried tarragon (crushed)
- sliced black olives
- Millet, Sprouted Sunflower Seeds and Dijon Mustard Sauce (p. 56)

METHOD:
1. Pre-heat oven to 425 or 450 degrees F. (depending upon your oven).
2. Saute carrots and cauliflower for a few minutes in water, white wine, or Vermouth until slightly tender.
3. Add onions and green peppers, sauteing briefly.
4. Turn off heat and add vinegar, sugar, and tarragon, stirring to mix the flavors throughout. Let cool to room temperature.
5. Using a slotted spoon, even spread stir-fried mixture onto the prepared and shaped dough.
6. Apply the topping sauce.
7. Sprinkle the top of the pizza with black olive slices.
8. Bake pizza for 15 to 20 minutes.

VARIATIONS:

- Sprinkled chopped or sliced nuts of choice on top of the pizza before baking.

NOTES:

- Recipe is for 1 12" to 14" pizza (1 lb. of dough).
- Inspired by the "Tarragon Vegetable Medley Recipe," in Better Homes and Gardens, "More from Your Wok," ISBN: 0-696-00765-7, 1982.

Gonzo Greens!

CRUST:

- Basic Pizza Dough (p. 14, using 1 cup semolina flour)

LAYERING INGREDIENTS:

- Quinoa, Artichoke Hearts, and Dijon Mustard Sauce (p. 61)
- 2 cups mixed chopped tender greens (arugula, romaine, radicchio, escarole, mustard, tender kale, young spinach, etc.)
- thinly sliced red onions (to taste)
- 1 T. of balsamic vinegar (to taste)
- 1/2 t. of sugar (optional)
- Parmiso (p. 90)
- ground pepper (optional)

METHOD:

1. Pre-heat oven to 425 or 450 degrees F. (depending upon your oven).
2. Top prepared and shaped dough with Quinoa, Artichoke Hearts, and Dijon Mustard Sauce.
3. Arrange sliced onions on top of pizza.
4. Bake pizza at 425 to 450 degrees F. for 10 minutes.
5. Mix greens with sugar and vinegar.
6. Remove pizza from oven, and arrange salad mixture on top of pizza.
7. Bake for another 5 to 10 minutes.
8. Sprinkle the pizza with Parmiso and ground pepper. Serve.

VARIATIONS:
- Sprinkle on sliced olives (black or green) on top of greens mixture before baking.

NOTES:
- Some might enjoy folding over slices of the pizza, New York-style, to eat them like a sandwich.

Asian Occasion

CRUST:
- Rice and Potato Crust (p. 22)

LAYERING INGREDIENTS:
- Oriental Sauce (p. 37)
- chopped spinach (raw or cooked, drained and squeezed)
- carrots (sliced thin diagonally)
- red and/or green peppers (julienned)
- snow peas
- sliced mushrooms
- Tofu and Sprouted Sunflower Seeds Sauce (p. 82, omit cumin)
- scallions (chopped)

METHOD:
1. Pre-heat oven to 425 or 450 degrees F. (depending upon your oven).
2. Spread Oriental Sauce over Rice and Potato Crust
3. Sprinkle on spinach.
4. Lightly stir-fry carrots, peppers, snow peas, and mushrooms in a small amount of water until crisp tender.
5. Drain, and let cool to room temperature.
6. Put vegetables on top of spinach.
7. Pour on Tofu and Sprouted Sunflower Seeds Sauce.
8. Sprinkle with scallions.
9. Bake pizza for 15 to 20 minutes.

VARIATIONS:
- Add drained baby corn.
- Add thin strips of peeled cut eggplant to stir-fried vegetables.

NOTES:
- If in a hurry, skip pre-soaking sunflower seeds, although the resulting sauce will be less "fluffy."

Resources

PLANT-BASED RECIPES:

NO-ADDED OIL:
- http://engine2diet.com/
- http://fatfreevegan.com/
- http://forksoverknives/category/recipes
- http://heart.kumu.org/
- http://vegetarian.about.com/od/fatfreeveganrecipes/FatFree_Vegan_Recipes.htm
- http://www.drmcdougall.com/recipeindex.html
- http://www.fatfree.com
- http://www.managercomplete.com/engine2/recipes.aspx
- http://www.pcrm.org/health/diets/recipes

GENERAL:
- http://www.allcreatures.org/recipes.html
- http://www.bryannaclarkgrogan.com
- http://www.cok.net/lit/recipes/
- http://www.globalvegankitchen.com
- http://www.peta.org/living/vegetarian-living/recipes/default.aspx
- http://www.veganchef.com
- http://www.vegandad.com
- http://www.vegankitchen.com
- http://www.vegweb.com

PLANT-BASED NUTRITION:

NO-ADDED OIL:
- http://fatfreevegan.com/fatfree-faqs/
- http://www.drmcdougall.com/misc/2007nl/aug/oils.htm
- http://www.engine2diet.com/~engine2/about_e2/FAQ
- http://www.heartattackproof.com/
- http://www.madcowboy.com/02_MCIview05.000.html

(Mad Cowboy Interview with Dr. Esselstyn)

- http://www.madcowboy.com/02_MCIview07.000.html

(Mad Cowboy Interview with Rip Esselstyn)

GENERAL:
- http://veganradio.com/
- http://www.cspinet.org/
- http://www.drmcdougall.com
- http://www.ivu.org
- http://www.notmilk.com
- http://www.tryveg.com/cfi/toc/
- http://www.veganoutreach.org/guide/what_to_eat.html
- http://www.vegnews.org
- http://www.vrg.org

ANIMAL ISSUES:
American Vegan Society
- www.americanvegan.org

Animal Concerns Community
- www.animalconcerns.org

Circle of Life
- www.circleoflife.org

Compassion Over Killing
- www.cok.net

Farm Animal Reform Movement
- www.farmusa.org

Farm Sanctuary
- www.farmsanctuary.org

Humane Society of the U.S.
- www.hsus.org

In Defense of Animals
- www.idausa.org

People for the Ethical Treatment of Animals
- http://www.peta.org

Physician's Committee for Responsible Medicine
- http://www.pcrm.com

PIZZA:
- http://celiacdisease.about.com/od/glutenfreefoodshoppin1/tp/Gluten-Free-Pizza-Crusts-Offer-Chance-To-Get-Creative.htm
- http://www.liveforpizza.com/2009/06/using-a-pizza-stone/
- http://www.wikihow.com/Use-a-Pizza-Stone

- https://en.wikipedia.org/wiki/History_of_pizza

DIGITAL VIDEO:

- Campbell, Dr. T. Colin
  "Meat and Dairy Cause Cancer:" (45 minutes)
  https://www.youtube.com/watch?v=yfsT-qYeqGM

- Esselstyn, Dr. Caldwell
  "Bill Clinton, Dr. Ornish, & Dr. Esselstyn on CNN:"
  http://engine2diet.com/the-daily-beet/cnns-wolf-blitzer-
  interviews-dr-esselstyn-\and-dr-ornish-clintons-nutrition-doctors/
  "Make Yourself Heart Attack Proof:" (1 hour)

  https://www.youtube.com/watch?v=AYTf0z_zVs0
  "Bill Clinton on Letterman Show (a fan of Dr. Esselstyn):"

  https://www.youtube.com/watch?v=aPpcBMwLg2Q
  "No Oil! Not Even Olive Oil!:"
  https://www.youtube.com/watch?v=b_o4YBQPKtQ

- Esselstyn, Rip
  "Rip on the Today Show:"
  https://www.youtube.com/watch?v=xLqa0Oea5t4

- Lyman, Howard
  "From 2010 - Talk: Plain Truth from the Cattle Rancher Who
  Won't Eat Meat:" (1 hour)
  https://www.youtube.com/watch?v=ZCMWctmCCqU

- McDougall, Dr. John

  "The Starch Solution:"

  https://www.youtube.com/watch?v=4XVf36nwraw

- Novick, RD, Jeff

  "Oil to Nuts: The Truth About Oils:"

  https://www.youtube.com/watch?v=lbALgjmZUek

DVDs:

- Grayer, Julia , director/producer, *Chowdown* (with Dr. Caldwell Esselstyn and others of note), 2010. http://chowdownmovie.com

- Lyman, Howard, *A Mad Cowboy Lecture - (2007)*. http://www.madcowboy.com

- McDougall, Dr. John, *Dr. McDougall's Common Sense Nutrition*. http://www.drmcdougall.com/books_tapes.html

- Monson, Shaun, writer/producer/director, *Earthlings* (2005). http://www.earthlings.com

- Rosow, Gene, and Bill Benenson, producers, *Dirt: The Movie*. http://www.dirtthemovie.org/

- Wendel, Brian, Creator and Executive Producer (starring Dr. T. Colin Campbell, Dr. Caldwell B. Esselstyn Jr., et al.), *Forks Over Knives*, (2011). http://www.forksoverknives.com

BOOKS OF NOTE:

Barnard, Dr. Neal, *21-Day Weight Loss Kickstart: Boost Metabolism, Lower Cholesterol, and Dramatically Improve Your Health* (Hachette Book Group, 2011). http://www.pcrm.org

___, *The Get Healthy, Go Vegan Cookbook: 125 Easy and Delicious Recipes to Jump-Start Weight Loss and Help You Feel Great* (Da Capo Lifelong Books, 2010).

___, *The Cancer Survivor's Guide* (Book Publishing Company, Summertown, Tenn., 2008).

___, (with Bryanna Clark Grogan), *Dr. Neal Barnard's Program for Reversing Diabetes*, (Rodale, 2007).

___, *Breaking the Food Seduction: The Hidden Reasons Behind Food Cravings - and 7 Steps to End Them Naturally* (St. Martin's Press, 2003).

Campbell, T. Colin, and Thomas M. Campbell, II, *The China Study* (Benbella Books, 2003). http://thechinastudy.com

Cambell, T. Colin, and Howard Jacobson, "WHOLE: Rethinking the Science of Ntrition." (Benbella Books, 2013).

Esselstyn, Jr., Dr. Caldwell, *Prevent and Reverse Heart Disease*, (Avery, 2007). http://www.heartattackproof.com

Esselstyn, Rip, *The Engine 2 Diet*, (Grand Central Publishing, 2009). http://engine2diet.com/

Foer, Jonathan Safran, *Eating Animals*, (Hachette Book Group, 2010). http://www.eatinganimals.com/

Goldhamer, Dr. Alan (ed.), *The Health Promoting Cookbook: Simple, Guilt-Free, Vegetarian Recipes* (Book Publishing Company, 1997). http://www.healthpromoting.com/

Lisle, Douglas J., and Alan Goldhamer, *The Pleasure Trap: Mastering the Hidden Force That Undermines Health & Happiness* (Healthy Living Publications, 2003). http://www.healthpromoting.com/

Lyman, Howard, with Merzer, Glen and Joanna Samorow-, *No More Bull! The Mad Cowboy Targets America's Worst Enemy: Our Diet* (Scribner, 2005). http://www.madcowboy.com
___, with Merzer, Glen, *Mad Cowboy: Plain Truth from the Cattle Rancher Who Won't Eat Meat* (Scribner, 1998).

Marcus, Erik, Vegan: The New Ethics of Eating, (McBooks Press , 2000). http://www.vegan.com

McDougall, Dr. John, *Dr. McDougall's Digestive Tune-Up* (Book Publishing Company, 2006). http://www.drmcdougall.com
___, *The McDougall Program for Women* (Plume, 2000)
___, *The McDougall Quick & Easy Cookbook* (Plume, 1999)
___, *The McDougall Program for a Healthy Heart* (Plume, 1998)
___, *The New McDougall Cookbook* (Plume, 1997)

Pollan, Michael, Food Rules, (Penguin Press, 2011)
___, *Omnivore's Dilemma*, (Penguin Press, 2009)

Regan, Tom, *Empty Cages: Facing the Challenge of Animal Rights* (Rowman & Littlefield, 2004). http://www.tomregan-animalrights.com

Robbins, John, *The Food Revolution*, (Conari Press, 2001). http://www.foodrevolution.com

BLOGS, LISTS, FORUMS, & NEWSLETTERS:
- http://engine2diet.com/forum/
- http://engine2diet.com/the-daily-beet/
- http://groups.yahoo.com/group/fatfree_vegan/
- http://groups.yahoo.com/group/Mad_Cowboy/
- http://veganfeastkitchen.blogspot.com/
- http://www.drmcdougall.com/newsletter.htm
- http://www.happyhealthylonglife.com/
- http://www.ivu.org/onlinenews.php
- http://www.meatoutmondays.org/index.php
- http://www.vegan.com
- http://www.vegparadise.com
- http://www.zenpawn.com/vegblog/

Online Mail-Order Sources
- http://www.healthy-eating.com/
- http://www.veganessentials.com/
- http://www.veganstore.com/
- http://www.vegefood.com/
- http://www.vrg.org/links/products.htm

Glossary

ARTICHOKES

Canned artichokes or artichoke hearts will work equally well for these recipes, but it's important that they are packed in water. They are available in all supermarkets. Trader Joe's offers an inexpensive version that has been most useful in developing the sauces in this book. In general, a 14 oz. can of artichoke hearts will yield 1 1/4 to 1 1/2 cups when drained and quartered.

BARLEY

For the purposes of the recipes in this book, only pearled barley is being used. Do not used pre-cooked barley as the results will be unpredictable (and nutritionally sub-optimal). Pearl barley is available in most supermarkets and health food stores.

BUCKWHEAT FLOUR

Often used in making bread or pancakes, buckwheat flour can be found in some supermarkets and most health food stores. It is gluten-free. Note: a buckwheat pancake mix contains more than just buckwheat flour and is not a suitable substitute for the real thing.

BRAGG'S AMINO ACIDS

Made of Non-GMO soy and contains 16 different amino acids. It's taste is reminiscent of soy sauce or Tamari, and can pretty much be used interchangeably with them in recipes. As with Tamarai and soy sauce, Bragg's is high in sodium if used in excess. It can be purchased at some mainstream grocery stores and all health food stores.

CHICKPEAS

Otherwise known as garbanzos or garbanzo beans, chickpeas are most notable as a key ingredient in making hummus. Can be purchased canned or uncooked from all supermarkets.

CHICKPEA FLOUR

Also known as "garbanzo flour," chickpea flour can be found in some supermarkets and most health food stores. Gluten-free.

CHILI GARLIC SAUCE

Comprised of ground chilies, garlic, and sometimes vinegar, garlic chili sauce is very popular in Chinese, Vietnamese, Korean, and Thai cuisines. It can be purchased in pretty much all supermarkets, with the highest quality and better ingredient varieties found in Asian grocery stores. The Thai version of the sauce, "sriracha," contains chili peppers, distilled vinegar, garlic, sugar, and salt.

CORIANDER

The leaves of the coriander herb are used in a variety of cuisines, most notably in the United States for making salsa. Coriander seeds can be purchased whole or as ground coriander (with a very aromatic taste). Available in just about all grocery stores.

CORN STARCH

Available in all grocery stores, corn starch is used as a thickening agent for topping sauce recipes in this book. Store covered in a refrigerator.

CUMIN

A very popular spice used primarily in Indian and Mexican cuisines. In seed form, it is particularly tasty lightly roasted before using. The seeds can be ground at home in a spice mill or ground cumin can be purchased at all supermarkets. Purchase bulk amounts from an Indian or Mexican grocery store for considerable savings.

CURRY POWDER

A very popular spice used primarily in South Asian (or Indian) cuisine. The best curry powder is homemade. Curry powder usually consists of coriander, turmeric, cumin, fenugreek, and red pepper. Some blends will contain other spices as well such as cinnamon, nutmeg, black pepper, and more. Easily obtained from most supermarkets with less expensive, bulk curry powder available in Indian or Pakistani grocery stores.

ENER-G

This is one of the first commercially available egg replacers. A white powder, it's largely made of potato starch and tapioca flour. Ener-G is available in some grocery stores and most health food stores. In general, for baking recipes, 1 1/2 t. of Ener-G mixed with 2 tablespoons of water is the equivalent of 1 egg. For the recipes in this book, cornstarch or ground flax seeds are not equal substitutes to Ener-G by amount.

FLAX SEEDS

Well-known for having a high Omega 3 content, people following a plant-based diet are generally advised to consume a tablespoon's worth of flax seeds daily. Available in most supermarkets and health food stores, when ground up (as meal) and mixed with water, they make an good egg substitute for baking as well as in sauces. The ratio of ground flax seeds to water (equivalent of one egg) is: 1 tablespoon of ground flax seeds mixed with 2 to 3 tablespoons of water.

GARAM MASALA

A very complex mixture of primarily Indian spices, garam masala is a staple in that cuisine and its composition varies from region to region. It is pungent, and small amounts are advised when using. Available in some grocery stores, most health food stores, and all Indian or Pakistani grocery stores, it's also quite easy to make from scratch for a more fragrant and delicate flavor:

http://homecooking.about.com/od/spicerecipes/r/blspice19.htm

GIMME LEAN SAUSAGE

Made by Lightlife, the Gimme Lean Sausage (and Hamburger) are superb zero fat low sodium vegan products. They (and other interesting faux meats, such as Gardein's products that would work well on pizzas) are available in many supermarkets and most health food stores. http://www.lightlife.com, http://www.gardein.com

GLUTEN-FREE

Many people are discovering that they have an allergic reaction to "gluten." Gluten is a protein found in wheat, barley, triticale, kamut, spelt, rye, and malts. Some of the gluten-free alternatives are rice, potatoes, tapioca, corn, millet, quinoa, and teff. For more information on gluten-free foodstuffs:

http://www.mayoclinic.com/health/gluten-free-diet/my01140

JULIENNE

A technique for cutting vegetables into long, thin strips resembling the thickness of shoestrings and around 2 to 2 1/2 inches in length.

HOISIN SAUCE

Often referred to as "Chinese barbeque sauce," hoisin a a fragrant and aromatic dark sauce used mostly in stir-fries and grilled dishes. There are many brands, but most usually contain at least fermented soy, vinegar, garlic, chilis, and sugar. Some also contain miso. Can be purchased in most grocery stores and all Asian grocery stores. A little goes a long way and you might want to adjust how much is used in a recipe to personal taste.

HOT DOGS

Yves makes a great no-fat version ("Yves Meatless Hot Dog") and Lightlife's best hot dog is the "Smart Dog" which is also fat-free.

KIM CHI

An extremely popular fermented dish from Korea made with various vegetables and seasonings. There are hundreds of varieties of kim chi. The most common will contain cabbage, radishes, ginger, garlic, scallions, salt, hot peppers, and dried red pepper. Most supermarket-purchased kim chi is totally plant-based, most purchased from a Korean grocery store is not (fish sauce). It takes 4 to 7 days to make kim chi at home, with just about all the time required being letting it sit, fermenting. Use a search engine to find recipes for making your own.

KOMBU

Also known as "dashima," kombu is a sea vegetable used primarily in Japanese cuisine to make dashi, a soup stock. Rich in many minerals, kombu imparts and "heavy" flavor to a broth. It is often added when cooking beans to improve the beans digestibility. Available in most grocery stores and health food stores, kombu should be rinsed free of salt before using. Store sealed in a cupboard.

LIQUID SMOKE

Used to simulate the taste of cured meats (like bacon and ham). It has a strong flavor and should only contain water and natural hickory smoke as ingredients. Available in all supermarkets.

MILLET

A grain (well, really a seed) with an amazing nutritional profile, millet is available in some supermarkets and pretty much all health food stores.

MISO

A popular fermented product in Japanese cusine, miso is generally made of fermented soybeans and a grain or legume (rice, barley, or chickpeas). It has a high salt content and comes in many varieties. For the recipes in this book, brown rice, barley, and similar "white" misos are used. Miso can be found in some supermarkets and all health food stores. It should be stored in the refrigerator as a "living" food.

MORI-NU TOFU

Inexpensive, aseptic-packed tofu that doesn't need refrigeration and has a very long shelf life. Available in many supermarkets in 12.3 oz. "boxes", most Asian grocery stores and health food stores. The preferred type for recipes in this book is "lite extra-firm." **http://www.morinu.com**

NUTRITIONAL YEAST

This is a not the same as Brewer's yeast or the yeast used to make bread products. It comes in yellow flakes (best) and a powder. Available in bulk at health food stores, it contains a lot of B vitamins, and in some cases, is fortified with B12. Used to impart a "cheesy-like" taste to recipes, I store my nutritional yeast in the freezer, although in a tightly sealed jar, it can be stored in the pantry for several months.

OATS

For the recipes in this book, do not use instant oats or oatmeal. Rolled oats are used to help make a thicker cheese-like sauce. There's an ongoing debate about whether oats are gluten-free or not, with the consensus largely being that they are, unless contaminated in the production process. Oats that are certified gluten-free can be found in some supermarkets and health food stores. Rolled oats can be found in all supermarkets.

OAT FLOUR

Used to make a gluten-free crust, oat flour can be purchased "pre-made" in some supermarkets and health food stores. It can easily be made at home by processing dry rolled oats to flour in a blender or food processor.

PAPRIKA

This is a spice made from grinding up dried peppers (both sweet and/or hot). The taste can range from mild to hot. For the recipes in this book, paprika is used in sauces as a coloring agent, and is also sprinkled on topping sauces for visual effect and general taste.

PIMENTOS

A type of cherry pepper what is sweeter than red bell pepper. Available in all grocery stores, pimentos are used in these recipes to impart an orange color to a topping sauce.

PLANT-BASED DIET

A diet consisting of only those foods originating as plants. Meat of any kind, including fish, milk, cheese, and eggs, are not part of a plant-based diet.

POTATO STARCH

Available in a few supermarkets and many health food stores. Useful in making gluten-free crusts. Potato flour is not the same product as potato starch. However, some companies will label potato starch as "potato starch flour" which is fine to use in this book's recipes.

QUINOA

Known for it's high protein content, quinoa is available in many supermarkets and pretty much all health food stores. It's become much more mainstream in the past five years and can usually be found "boxed" in most grocery or health food stores. Most cooks advise rinsing quinoa and letting it drain before cooking. Although either red or white quinoa will work in these recipes, white provides a more conventional color to a topping sauce.

RICE FLOUR

Milled rice flour is available in some supermarkets and most health food stores. It can be used to make a gluten-free pizza crust.

SESAME SEEDS

Found primarily in pale or black versions, sesame seeds are a popular and nutritious condiment. They develop a marvelous nutty flavor when lightly roasted and are often blended in large amounts to make tahini, a primary ingredient in conventional hummus. However, sesame seeds are high in fat, and when concentrated into tahini, the resulting nut butter is not considered a Heart Healthy ingredient in this book. Sprinkled on a pizza (or used in "Parmiso (p. 90)" they provide negligible additional fat to any recipe. Available in most supermarkets and health food stores.

SHIITAKE MUSHROOMS
Popular in Asian Cuisine, shiitake mushrooms are known for their rich flavor and reported medicinal properties. They can be purchased raw or dried, with either being used in these recipes. Depending upon where you live, shiitake mushrooms can be purchased in supermarkets or health food stores (the best prices, though, will be at an Asian grocery store). Dried shiitake mushrooms will need to be hydrated in liquid of choice (usually water, sometimes sake!) until they soften. A quick method is to cover them with water in a small saucepan, bring to a boil, cover the saucepan, and let simmer 20 to 30 minutes until tender. The leftover broth is an excellent and nutritious addition to soups and sauces.

SPICE MILL
Used to grind spices or seeds in to a fine powder. A dedicated coffee bean grinder can also be very effective for grinding spices.

SUNFLOWER SEEDS
Ironically, these are not "seeds" but rather the fruit of the sunflower plant! They will swell up from soaking in water (imparting a creamy texture to a sauce) and can also be sprouted. Use only raw and unsalted sunflower seeds for Heart Healthy pizzas.

SWEETENERS
Agave nectar, maple syrup, or molasses, can all be used as an alternative sweetener to sugar. They can be found in most grocery stores and all health food stores.

TABASCO SAUCE

This hot sauce is made from hot peppers, vinegar, salt, and aged for a few years. There are many varieties available. For the purpose of recipes in this book, "Tabasco sauce" is a generic term for any "hot sauce" with a wide variety of taste and heat profiles.

TAMARI

A fermented wheat and/or soy sauce popular in Asia and available in most supermarkets. There are many varieties and for the purpose of this book, soy sauce can be used in place of Tamari. Heart Healthy cooks should consider using only "low sodium" versions of Tamari or soy sauce. Avoid cheap soy sauces that contain hydrolyzed vegetable protein and caramel coloring. Bragg's Amino Acids is an adequate substitute for Tamari or soy sauce, and isn't fermented. All three sauces are available in most grocery stores and all health food stores.

TEMPEH

A fermented soy bean product available in some supermarkets and most health food stores. Notorious for being able to soak up the flavor of a good marinade. Tempeh has a unique "spongy" texture and freezes well. Store tightly wrapped in the refrigerator. There are many varieties of tempeh (my personal favorite is a multi-grain tempeh), and as long as the tempeh is uncooked and not marinaded when purchased, it will be suitable for these recipes.

TOFU

Fermented soybean curd (tofu) is available in many varieties. Recipes in this book are using extra firm or lite extra firm tofu that has been drained and not pressed. Firm, soft, or silky tofu could be used instead, but care would have to be taken possibly using less water when making a cheese-like sauce. Extra firm is recommended. Tofu is stored in water in the refrigerator, changing the water minimally every other day. Tofu freezes well, but due to the spongey texture change when frozen and thawed, frozen tofu should not be used in the topping sauce recipes. Mori-Nu makes an excellent lite extra-firm tofu that is packaged in such a way it can be stored, initially, in your pantry for several months, making it quite convenient to have around for a quick meal. Tofu, if unpackaged, should be stored, covered, in water, changing the water periodically.

TRADER JOE'S

A unique "boutique" grocery store of sorts in the United States, TJ's was most useful during many of the recipe testing phases of this book. Key products (not including produce) from TJ's that are of note: the pre-made white, whole wheat, and white/basil 1 lb. pizza doughs, vegan cocktail sauce, Gimme Lean Sausage, water-packed artichokes, frozen roasted multi-color peppers, killer Dijon mustard, and the marvelous inexpensive wines (in some States). **http://www.traderjoes.com**

TURMERIC

A dark orange-yellow powder, turmeric has a earthy and bitter taste, and is reputed to aid in digesting legumes. Too much turmeric in a recipe will stain white utensils if they are not soaped down and rinsed immediately after preparation. For recipes in this book, turmeric imparts a slight orange color to a cheese-like sauce. Available in most supermarkets, health food stores, and in Indian or Pakistani stores.

TVP

Texturized (textured) vegetable protein is a defatted soy flour product that, when hydrated, resembles meat. It's availabe as granules, flakes, strips, chunks, and "breasts." Can be found in some grocery stores and most health food stores (and in bulk). Available at many shops online.

WET MUSTARD

More conventionally known as "prepared mustard" to distinguish it from dry mustard, wet mustard is a ground up mixture of mustard seeds, vinegar, and various other ingredients depending upon the variety. Favorites include: Chipotle, Dijon (and even with this type, has a high range of taste differences), Spicy Brown, Stone Ground, and Classic. Mustard is used in recipes primarily for taste and a tad for color. Types of mustards are interchangeable in these recipes.

WHITE BEANS

For the purposes of the recipes in this book, white beans are synonymous with white kidney beans, great northern beans, and navy beans.

YELLOW DAL

Yellow split peas are generically referred to as "dal" in the United States. They can be found in many supermarkets, all Indian or Pakistani grocery stores, and most health food stores. As cooked in one of the recipes in this book, they provide a nice velvety texture, in addition to significant fiber and overall nutrition. It is always important before cooking to carefully rinse uncooked dal and pick out any unwanted small pebbles.

YVES

Many faux meat products are high in fat and sodium, definitely not heart healthy. Yves is unique in that most of their products are either no-fat or extremely low in fat. Particularly notable in making Heart Healthy pizzas are their pepperoni and canadian bacon products (both fat-free), which when cooked on a pizza, are very hard to distinguish from the original meat-based products. You can buy these "meats" in most supermarkets and health food stores.

http://www.yvesveggie.com

Appendix 1: Reasons For Choosing A Plant-Based Diet

"The Gods created certain kinds of beings to replenish our bodies;
they are the trees and the plants and the seeds."

--- Plato

There are many reasons that people choose a solely plant-based diet. The following is a short summary of the main issues. Resource links to more information online for each can be found in the "Resources" section of this book.

HEALTH

Plant-based diets have been shown in numerous and detailed studies to be more nutritious, provide more antioxidants and phytochemicals, fiber, and a host of health giving assets missing from meat, fish, and dairy. People on this type of diet have been shown to generally live longer with less degenerative diseases, including heart disease, obesity, Type II diabetes, and various cancers. Even the conserative American Dietetic Association and Harvard Medical School have made major proclamations testifying to safety, nutritional benefits, and biological protective nature of a plant-based diet.

Furthermore, many people believe that our factory-farmed meat and dairy are host to a plethora of unnecessary hormones, antibiotics, and food borne diseases. It's also well known that ocean fish can contain high levels of dioxins and that most of the fresh water fish in the United States have high concentrations of mercury (even the Federal Drug Agency has warned pregnant women about consuming fresh water fish).

Another reason to consider avoiding animal protein is the convincing findings by Dr. T. Colin Campbell, director of the largest study on diet in history, "The China Study," indicating that it enables the development of cancer and promotes heart disease.

However, a plant-based diet can also be very unhealthy if comprised of a lot of fried, salty, sugary and highly-processed food-like products. It is advisable to incorporate a lot of fresh vegetables, fruits, greens, legumes, and whole grains into one's diet, and that by minimizing consumption of processed foods and maximizing diversity in what we eat, the health benefits for our bodies and minds are optimized.

ENVIRONMENT

Some people are focused on the issue of how deleterious modern meat, dairy, and farmed fish production is on our environment. A significant portion of the greenhouse gases being emitted into our atmosphere comes directly from cows. Concerns over the incredible amount of manure produced by these factory farms are also mentioned, and that even some of our rivers and bays are now too polluted from the runoff from these farms to swim in without risking one's health. Also, the amount of land being wasted to grow specific and mono-cultured plants to service factory farmed animals is land that can't be used to benefit humans in a less resource-intensive manner and maintain a robust natural ecology.

There's also the problem of how much oil is being used in factory farming (in the form of petroleum), and concerns that these animal congested farms are breeding grounds for diseases shown to jump from animal species to humans (avian flu is an example). Furthermore, a strong case can be made that the amount of water and food being fed to these animals is excessive and wasteful in a society where natural resources are becoming scarcer. It's also well known that the astounding amount of antibiotics utilized to fight disease in factory animals (caused from the appalling living conditions and bad diet) is contributing directly to antibiotic resistance in humans, meaning that several of our own important disease fighters are becoming less and less effective.

In summary: factory farming is wasteful of many important resources, severely pollutes the environment in many ways, and is having a direct negative impact on our collective health.

ANIMAL ISSUES

There is no question that factory-farmed animals live a brutal, cruel, and sad life. These poor creatures are tortured and force-fed foods they are not designed to consume, mutilated (in the case of fowl and pigs), crowded and trapped in extremely small spaces compared to how they would live in the wild, and often slaughtered painfully. Many people take offense to this treatment of another life form, ranging from those wanting the process to be more humane to those wanting these heinous practices abolished, period.

For some, eating meat, dairy, and fish contributes to an industry they find offensive and believe that in consuming these dead animals they themselves are morally culpable. They believe that as non-human life forms continue to increasingly show via ongoing scientific research, far more intellectual, emotional, and conscious awareness of "self" than originally thought possible, these animals have rights and deserve more compassion and respect from humans.

Whether animals are being killed for food, clothing, or other products, it's considered by those concerned with these animal issues to be a wrongful exploitation of creatures who are unable to speak in their own defense.

SPIRITUALITY

There are many who believe, philosophically and spiritually, that life is sacred and that the killing of animals is an affront to the power or powers that be and that our spiritual obligation is to take proper care of these living gifts. Some also believe that there's a strong negative effect on one's spiritual or physical nature in the eating of dead flesh. Finally, many think that by eating a solely plant-based diet, one's consciousness is raised and a lot of negative karma eliminated via more positive energies.

"Eat food. Not too much. Only plants."

--- Mark Sutton (paraphrasing Michael Pollen)

Appendix 2: The Problems With Added Oil Or Fat

"Really, this [heart] disease is kind of a paper tiger. Chronic heart disease is not inevitably progressive, like cancer, this is something that really can be changed, can be changed drastically when you make significant changes in the nutritional profile."
--- Dr. Caldwell Esselstyn

The quote above is from my February 2007 interview with Dr. Esselstyn. Howard Lyman, aka, "The Mad Cowboy," suggested that I interview Dr. Esselstyn about his research and his new book, "Prevent and Reverse Heart Disease." Howard explained that Esselstyn had successfully reversed heart disease in very ill heart patients (something no one in conventional modern medicine has accomplished). He did this by having his patients maintain a no-added oil plant-based diet and he believes through such we can effectively "heart attack proof" ourselves. It's worth noting that on the other side of the country, on the West Coast, Dr. Dean Ornish was, independently, obtaining similar results. Individually, their research has survived well over 20 years of peer-review. These are very important and significant findings, for as Dr. Esselstyn points out: "In the course of a lifetime, one out of every two American men and one out of every three American women will have some form of the disease."

As editor of the Mad Cowboy e-newsletter, I was delighted by the opportunity to chat with Dr. Esselstyn, but as the son of a man who'd just had a major heart event, I was driven to punch as hard as I could during the interview, and come up with every argument I could think of to find a crack or flaw in his approach. He relished the discussion and convinced me completely that the diet he was advocating was important and worthy of serious attention. He also insisted that a person could lose their taste addiction to fat and "re-calibrate" one's taste buds after about 14 or so weeks of avoiding added oil. Already on a plant-based diet, I went no-added fat shortly after the interview. For nearly five years now, I've been added fat free and have completely lost my taste for added fat.

Why no added oil? There are a myriad of reasons and research indicating that high-fat food is not healthy, but here are some of the key points related to Dr. Esselstyn's and other's research:

- Dr. Robert Vogel at the University of Maryland has definitively measured the impact on the lining of one's arteries (the endothelium) of consuming oil. The oil (or even one high-fat meal) affects the elasticity of the arteries, and often for several hours until they return to normal. This recurring biological insult to the circulatory system eventually takes it's negative toll.

- Added oil directly fuels development of the type of plaque that causes over 90% of strokes. By not feeding the plaque, a major heart disease enabler is eliminated.

- As Dr. John McDougall has pointed out, vegetable oils are not real food. They promote "free radicals" in your body that also damage the lining of your arteries.

- Jeff Novick, R.D., points out that oil is the most calorie-dense "food" on the planet, and is higher in fat content than equivalent amounts of bacon or butter.

- Dr. Neal Barnard has successfully reversed Type II Diabetes in patients through a no-added oil plant-based diet.

- Research by Dr. Dean Ornish has indicated that a low-fat plant-based diet led to increased levels of telomerase, an enzyme that protects and repairs DNA.

There are many misconceptions and myths about the health benefits of oil. There are links to information discussing these issues and to sites with recipes devoted to this type of diet in the "Resources" section of this book.

However, there is one myth that bears mentioning in this summary: the issue of moderation. Esselstyn, Barnard, and McDougall are all clear on this point: there is no success in moderation, and it's one of the reasons people's health in this country continues to deteriorate. Moderation doesn't help and doesn't get to the root of the problem. Besides, why feed and promote an addiction? With a little discipline and effort anyone can enjoy the health and protective benefits of a no-added fat plant-based diet.

"We should be aiming much higher: at arresting coronary artery disease altogether, even reversing its course. And the key to doing this, as my research demonstrates, is not simply reducing the amount of fat and cholesterol you ingest, but eliminating cholesterol and any fat beyond the natural, healthy amounts found in plants, from your diet. The key is plant-based nutrition." --- Dr. Caldwell Esselstyn ("Prevent and Reverse Heart Disease," p. 37).

Appendix 3: Fat Stats For Plant-Based Cheeses

"...Many people get hooked on cheese. Like other dairy products, cheese contains casein, a protein that breaks apart during digestion to form opiates, called casomorphins."

--- Dr. Neal Barnard (in, "Breaking the Food Seduction")

Although the current generation of plant-based faux cheese are often remarkable in their taste and texture profile (to the point of really being "gooey"), what's often not recognized by those who praise them is that for the most part, these products are high in fat. They are generally nutritionally useless with most of the fat coming from added oil and or a large amount of nuts.

In researching the amount of fat per serving for the products below it was surprising how many of the websites for these products do not have the actual nutritional information for those products available online. Again and again one can read about "how healthy" these products are and about all the things they don't have in them, yet how much fat per serving isn't mentioned. They tend to define their product by what it doesn't contain, versus the as important, "what is it made of?" Most are nutritionally useless.

Dr. Caldwell Esselstyn (author, "Prevent and Reverse Heart Disease") has successfully reversed heart disease in many patients through a no-added fat plant-based diet. Twenty plus years of peer-reviewed research on his work (and Dr. Dean Ornish's) is hard to ignore.

Esselstyn recommends a total of around 15 to 25 grams of fat, per day, for the average adult. None of this fat should come from added oil, including that in plant-based cheeses.

The following list is of two dairy cheeses and the most popular plant-based cheeses (with the exception of the Galaxy products). All measurements are for 1/4 cup (one serving). The first number is the approximate amount of fat grams per serving and second number is the approximate percentage of total fat recommended per day (as recommended by Dr. Esselstyn) this fat amount represents.

Dairy Cheddar Cheese (shredded), 10 grams, 40%
Dairy Whole Milk Mozzarella Cheese, 6 grams, 24%

Daiya Cheddar Shreds, 6 grams, 24%
Daiya Mozzarella Shreds, 6 grams, 24%

Dr. Cow Dairy-Free Aged Cashew and Brazil Nut Cheese, 10.5 grams, 42%
Dr. Cow Dairy-Free Aged Cashew and Hemp Cheese, 10.5 grams, 42%

Sheese Mozzarella, 10 grams, 40%
Sheese Cheddar, 10 grams, 40%

Follow Your Heart Vegan Mozzarella, 7 grams, 28%
Follow Your Heart Vegan Cheddar, 7 grams, 28%

Galaxy Foods Rice Mozzarella, 3 grams, 12%
Galaxy Foods Rice Cheddar, 3 grams, 12%

Teese Mozzarella Cheese, 6 grams, 24%
Teese Cheddar Cheese, 6 grams, 24%

Vegan Rella Soy Cheese, 6 grams, 24%

It's worth noting that all of them but two, have as much or more fat per serving as whole milk mozzarella. Hardly "low fat" products as some of their makers claim. This is one of the primary reasons for writing "Heart Healthy Pizza": to provide a healthy alternative to these expensive nutritionally useless faux food products.

Those believing that cheese analogs are a solution for people on a plant-based diet who miss dairy cheese may not understand the true nature of the problem. Added fat is added fat, it's addictive, and it's not good for human cardiovascular systems nor many other aspects of a person's body.

Even in "moderation."

Appendix 4: Cooking Grains & Legumes

"Then God said, "I give you every seed-bearing plant on the face of the whole earth and every tree that has fruit with seed in it. They will be yours for food."

--- Genesis 1:29

The two major techniques for cooking whole grains are the Stovetop Method and using a Pressure Cooker:

STOVETOP METHOD:

Grains are rinsed if necessary and put into a stovetop pot with an amount of water based upon the type of grain (see below). The grains and water are brought to a boil, covered, and simmered on very low until the water is dried up. The grains may be fluffed up with a fork, and then allowed to sit covered until coming to room temperature.

Toasting grains before cooking involves sauteing them in a dry skillet until they start to get toasty. This preparation makes for a nutty flavor when the grain is cooked (particularly when using millet or barley).

With the exception of millet and quinoa, to cut down on cooking time grains can be soaked overnight, rinsed and drained again. This will reduce cooking time down about 15 minutes.

All the topping sauce recipes in this book using grains use whole grains. Enriched pre-cooked rice doesn't take full advantage of the nutritional values in rice and may easily effect the final viscosity of any topping sauce and is definitely not recommended.

Spices can also be added before turning on the heat to cook whole grains, and certainly different combinations of liquids can be used (including, but not limited to, vegetable broth, white wine, and beer).

USING A PRESSURE COOKER:

Grains are rinsed if necessary and put into a pressure cooker with an amount of water twice the amount of grain (note: the mixture should not exceed the pressure cooker being half full). Seal lid cover tightly, bring to high pressure, then drop to low to maintain pressure for time indicated. Remove from heat and wait five minutes. Gradually open the release valve (or if using a pressure cooker with a dial gauge, the steam vent). If the grain is not cooked completely, seal cover, bring to high temperature, drop to low, and cook another five minutes. Remove from heat, wait five minutes, check again. Repeat if necessary.

Some people believe it's not advisable to use a pressure cooker to cook millet or quinoa. Not only do they already cook up pretty quickly as it is, the small grains might clog up the pressure cooker's valves depending upon the type of pressure cooker.

Pearl barley and rice are the two grains in this book that would benefit best from pressure cooking.

As there are different types of pressure cookers, it's <u>very important that the cook should review the owner's manual carefully for advice on how to cook grains with that particular device.</u> The above suggestions are general and different pressure cookers may have different requirements for safe and proper usage.

GRAINS, LIQUID, COOKING TIME, AND YIELD (for 1 cup):

Pearl Barley (not hulled):
Stovetop: 3 cups water, 40 to 45 minutes, 3 cups.
Pressure Cooker: 4 cups water, 15 to 20 minutes, 3 cups.

Millet::
Stovetop: 2 to 2 1/4 cup water, 15 to 20 minutes, 3 cups.

Quinoa:
Stovetop: 2 to 2 1/4 cups water, 15 to 20 minutes, 3 cups.

Rice:
Stovetop: 2 to 2 1/4 cups water, 40 to 45 minutes, 3 cups yield.
Pressure Cooker: 1 1/4 to 1 1/2 cup water, 15 minutes, 3 cups yield.

NOTE:
Amounts of water and yield vary sometimes due to cooking heat, type of pot (or pressure cooker), and grain measurement. For the recipes in this book, it's best not to overcook grains. If, as an example, more water than indicated is used for millet, it gets quite soft and mushy (millet polenta!).

COOKING LEGUMES:

As with grains, there are two preferred methods for cooking beans:

STOVETOP METHOD:

Beans are rinsed and soaked overnight, rinsed and drained in the morning for later use (they can be stored, covered, in the refrigerator). The exceptions to this technique are the very small beans, like lentils (not used in this book for topping sauces) and yellow dal (which is used). In this book we are using black beans, black-eyed peas, white beans, cannellini beans, chickpeas, lima beans, great northern beans, and pinto beans.

The general technique is essentially the same as with grains, only the goal is a tender bean and not worrying about all the water being evaporated. Beans are put in the pot with suggested water amount (no salt), brought to a boil, stirred, covered, and brought to a simmer on very low heat. Simmer for appropriate length of time. Check to see if tender, if not, simmer longer. If tender, remove from heat and drain.

The fast soak method of cooking beans is to add beans and measured amount of water to a covered pot, bring to a boil, turn off the heat, and let sit, covered and undisturbed for at least an hour. Drain, and cook using by the stovetop method above.

PRESSURE COOKING:

Beans are rinsed, added to pressure cooker with measured water. Top is securely sealed, and pressure brought up to around 15 lbs., temperature lowered to maintain pressure. Heat is turned off and pressure cooker is opened after pressure has dropped to zero lbs.

It is not necessary to pre-soak beans beforehand when using a pressure cooker, although some people do.

For the beans listed above, use 4 cups of water for 1 cup of beans, for 5 to 8 minutes on high pressure. Yield with be between 2 and 2 1/2 cups depending upon the type and size of the bean used.

As there are different types of pressure cookers, it's <u>very important that the cook should review the owner's manual carefully for advice on how to cook beans with that particular device.</u> The above suggestions are general.

BEANS, LIQUID, COOKING TIME, AND YIELD:
Stovetop Method (for 1 cup of beans):

Black Beans: 4 cups water, 45 minutes to 1 1/4 hours, 2 1/4 cups.
Black-eyed Peas: 3 cups water, 45 minutes to 1 hour, 2 cups.
Cannellini (white kidney beans): 3 cups water, 35 to 45 minutes, 2 1/2 cups.
Garbanzos (chickpeas): 4 cups water, 1 to 1 1/2 hours, 2 cups.
Great Northern Beans: 3 cups water, 1 to 1 1/2 hours, 2 1/2 cups.
Lima Beans: 4 cups water, 45 minutes to 1 hour, 2 to 2 1/2 cups.
Navy Beans: 3 cups water, 45 minutes to 1 1/4 hours, 2 1/2 cups.
Pinto Beans: 3 cups water, 45 minutes to 1 1/4 hours, 2 /2 cups.

Cooking time and yield for beans will vary depending upon the size of the bean and it's freshness before soaking.

Recipes Index

CHAPTER 1: FIRM FOUNDATIONS
Basic Pizza Dough..14
Whole Wheat Dough..15
Pumpernickel or Rye Dough..15
Wheat and Millet Dough..16
Wheat and Black Bean Dough...17
Corn Polenta...17
Millet Polenta..18
Whole Grain Rice and Chickpea Flour..19
Buckwheat and Chickpea Flour Crust...20
Oat Flour Crust...21
Rice and Potato Crust...22

CHAPTER 2: AMAZING GRACIOUS SAUCES
Classic Tomato Sauce...25
Raw Tomato Sauce..26
Quick Italian Tomato Sauce...27
Red Tomato Salsa...27
Carrot Sauce...28
Tangy Blenderized BBQ Sauce...29
Thousand Island Dressing Sauce..30
Basil Pesto..30
Rosemary Pesto..31
Green Tomato Salsa..31
Mucho Mocko Guaco...32
Lite Light Brown-White Sauce...33
Tofu Ricotta...34
Polynesian Sauce..34
Indian Spice White Sauce...35
Corn Comfort Sauce..36
Mark's Mashed-Up Potatoes Sauce..36
Oriental Sauce...37

CHAPTER 3: NO NONSENSE NON-CHEESE SAUCES
Barley and Almonds Sauce...46
Barley, White Beans, and Horseradish Sauce.....................................47
Barley, Carrot, and Potato Sauce..48
Barley, Carrot, Sunflower Seeds, and Chili Garlic Sauce....................49
Barley, Mushrooms, and Tofu Sauce...49
Barley, Cauliflower, and Vermouth Sauce..50

Millet, Avocado, and Oregano Sauce...51

Millet, Black-eyed Peas, and Ginger Sauce...52
Millet, Cashews, and Mustard Sauce..53
Millet, Oats, and Cashews Sauce..53
Millet, Quinoa, and Flax Seeds Sauce...54
Millet, Sunflower Seeds, and Oregano Sauce...55
Sprouted Millet, Flax Seeds, and Cashews..55
Millet, Sprouted Sunflower Seeds and Dijon Mustard..56

Oats, Mustard, and Nutritional Yeast Sauce..57
Oats, Cannellini Beans, and Garlic Sauce...58
Oats, Cauliflower, and Carrot Sauce..59
Oats, Carrot, and Corn Sauce...59
Oats, Pinto Beans, and Salsa Sauce..60

Quinoa, Artichoke Hearts, and Dijon Mustard Sauce..61
Quinoa, Artichoke Hearts, and Sunflower Seeds Sauce..62
Quinoa, Carrots, and Corn Sauce...62
Quinoa, Cauliflower, Almonds, and Garlic Sauce...63
Quinoa and Colored Sweet Peppers Sauce...64
Quinoa, Lima Beans, and Walnuts Sauce...65
Quinoa, Sweet Potato, and Corn Sauce...65
Quinoa, Tofu, and Flax Seeds Sauce..66

Rice, Cannellini Beans, and Almonds Sauce..67
Rice and Cauliflower Sauce..68
Rice, Oats, and Cashews Sauce...68
Rice and Sunflower Seeds Sauce...69
Rice, Chickpeas, and Corn Sauce..70

Chickpeas, Oats, and Pimentos Sauce..72
Lima Beans, Millet, and Flax Seed Sauce 72
Navy Beans, Rice, and Fresh Basil Sauce...73
Great Northern Beans, Millet, and Cashew Sauce...74
White Beans and Millet Sauce..75
Cannellini Beans, Oregano, and Walnut Sauce..75
Navy Beans and Pecans Sauce..76
Yellow Dal and Rice Sauce...76

Tofu, Basil, and White Wine Sauce...78
Tofu and Lemon Sauce...79
Tofu and Rice Sauce...80
Tofu and Millet Sauce...80
Tofu, Millet, and Cocktail Sauce Sauce..81
Tofu, Dill, and Dijon Mustard Sauce...82
Tofu and Sprouted Sunflower Seeds Sauce...82
Cauliflower, Carrots, and Black-eyed Peas Sauce...83

Cauliflower, Millet, and Carrot Sauce..84
Potato, Carrot, and Ginger Sauce...85
Sweet Potato, Oats, Carrot, and Green Chili Sauce...86

CHAPTER 4: POWERFUL PIZZA POSSIBILITIES

Pizza Margherita..89
Parmiso..90
Pizza Putanesca with Tempeh Anchovies..91
Tempeh Anchovies..91
Pizza Genovese..92
Pizza Florentine..93
Pizza Fungi...94
TVP Sausage..95
Pizza Norma...96
Pizza Caponata...97
Pizza Corn Polenta..98
Nearly Nouveaux Mex...99
Southwestern Special..99
The Official Mad Cowboy...101
Thymely Summer Squash..101
Friendly Frankfurters & Kale..102
Artsy Artichoke, Mushroom, and Corn...103
Sausage, Broccoli, and Mushrooms...104
Sauteed Gimme Lean Sausage..104
Over the Rainbow Chard..104
Stir-fried Greens Recipe...105
Terrific Tri-Pepper...106
Jumbo Gingered Gumbo..107
Really Reubenesque...109
Powerful Pepperoni and Mushroom..109
Roasty Veggielicious..110
Roasting Vegetables Method..111
Gratefully Greek..112
Tofu Feta Cheese..113
Spanakopizza..114
Krazy Kim Chi Please...115
Pleasing Polynesian...115
St. Patty's Pizza Pie..116
TVP Corned Beef Cubes..117
Indian Samosa-Styled Pizza...118
Clever Curry..119
Vivid Vegetable Tarragon...120
Gonzo Greens!..121
Asian Occasion..122

General Index

B
Beans..

    Black Beans.. 17, 160, 161
    Black Eyed Peas...52, 83, 84, 108, 160, 161
    Cannellini beans...58, 67, 75, 93, 160
    Chickpeas..70, 72, 120, 134, 138, 160, 161
    Great Northern Beans...67, 74, 75, 144, 160, 161
    Lima Beans...65, 72, 73, 103, 160, 161
    Navy Beans...67, 71, 73, 74, 76, 144, 161
    Pinto Beans..60, 99, 100, 101, 160, 161
    White beans...47, 75, 91, 98, 105, 115, 116, 144, 160
    White kidney beans..58, 71, 75, 144, 161
    Yellow dal.. 76, 77, 144, 160

C
Corn starch.35, 36, 37, 38, 40, 46, 47, 48, 50, 51, 52, 53, 54, 55, 56, 57, 60, 61, 62, 64, 65, 66, 68, 69, 70, 72, 73, 74, 75, 76, 77, 78, 79, 80, 81, 82, 84, 85, 86, 92, 134

E
Ener-G...29, 31, 40, 49, 58, 59, 60, 63, 65, 67, 83, 135

F
Flax seeds. .19, 20, 21, 22, 28, 36, 40, 50, 54, 55, 56, 59, 60, 62, 63, 64, 66, 67, 72, 73, 90, 135

Fruits...

    Coconut.. 115, 116, 119
    Lemon....26, 30, 31, 32, 33, 34, 35, 51, 57, 61, 62, 63, 64, 68, 73, 75, 76, 77, 78, 79, 80, 82, 91
    Lime...31, 32, 33, 34, 59, 64
    Pineapple...29, 34, 101, 115
    Raisins...26, 105, 119

G
Grains...

    Barley.......15, 41, 45, 46, 47, 48, 49, 50, 94, 105, 116, 133, 136, 138, 143, 157, 158, 159
    Buckwheat...20

Millet.16, 18, 19, 41, 45, 51, 52, 53, 54, 55, 56, 72, 73, 74, 75, 80, 81, 84, 89, 91, 97, 99, 100, 102, 103, 104, 108, 115, 116, 119, 120, 136, 138, 157, 158, 159

Oats..........................21, 41, 45, 53, 57, 58, 59, 60, 68, 69, 72, 86, 93, 101, 110, 138, 139

Quinoa.............45, 46, 54, 61, 62, 63, 64, 65, 66, 100, 107, 121, 136, 140, 157, 158, 159

Rice....15, 19, 22, 34, 37, 41, 46, 67, 68, 69, 70, 73, 74, 76, 77, 80, 96, 97, 98, 110, 115, 122, 136, 138, 140, 141, 143, 154, 155, 157, 158, 159

H
Herbs...

Basil...........10, 25, 26, 27, 28, 29, 30, 40, 70, 73, 74, 78, 79, 89, 90, 92, 93, 98, 113, 143

Cilantro...27, 28, 31, 32, 33

Coriander...37, 100, 118, 119, 134, 135

Dill..44, 82, 85, 116

Italian..19, 21, 26, 27, 70, 178

Marjoram...26, 98

Oregano...........26, 32, 36, 51, 55, 59, 60, 68, 72, 73, 75, 89, 97, 100, 107, 108, 110, 112

Parsley...26, 27, 29, 31, 33, 35, 116, 119

Rosemary...26, 31, 93, 94, 101

Tarragon...50, 51, 73, 120, 121

Thyme...94, 95, 101, 102, 104, 107, 108, 114

M
Miscellaneous...

Condiments...

Cocktail sauce...81, 82, 143

Garlic sauce...38, 49, 58, 63, 93, 134

Hoisin sauce...37, 38, 136

Ketchup...35, 82, 117

Kim Chi...50, 75, 115, 137

Liquid smoke...29, 95, 137

Mustard 40, 42, 47, 50, 51, 52, 53, 54, 56, 57, 59, 61, 62, 64, 66, 69, 72, 74, 75, 76, 78, 80, 82, 83, 84, 86, 99, 102, 103, 104, 107, 116, 120, 121, 143, 144

Parmiso...89, 90, 92, 93, 94, 96, 98, 112, 121, 140

Pickle..30, 102, 103

Salsa...3, 24, 27, 28, 31, 32, 60, 61, 101, 134

Tabasco sauce.....26, 32, 40, 48, 50, 52, 54, 58, 61, 64, 65, 67, 72, 83, 84, 95, 100, 108, 117, 141

Tamari.................................25, 37, 91, 92, 94, 95, 104, 105, 106, 111, 113, 133, 142

Meat/Dairy Analogs...

Gimme Lean Sausage...94, 104, 136, 143

Pepperoni...109, 110, 144

Tempeh Anchovies..91
Tofu Feta Cheese... 112, 113, 114
Tofu hot dogs..102
TVP.. 94, 95, 96, 104, 105, 116, 117,143
TVP Corned Beef Cubes...116, 117
TVP Sausage...94, 95, 104, 105

Recipes...
    Parmiso Recipe..90
    Roasting Vegetables Method...111
    Sauteed Gimme Lean Sausage Recipe...104
    Stir-fried Greens Recipe...105
    Tempeh Anchovies Recipe...91
    Tofu Feta Cheese Recipe..113
    TVP Corned Beef Cubes Recipe..117
    TVP Sausage Recipe..95
Miso...28, 30, 33, 47, 67, 137, 138

N
Nutritional yeast26, 27, 30, 33, 34, 37, 40, 42, 46, 50, 51, 52, 53, 54, 55, 56, 57, 58, 59, 60, 63, 65, 67, 68, 69, 70, 72, 73, 75, 76, 79, 80, 81, 82, 90, 97, 112, 113, 114, 138

Nuts..
    Almond... 34, 41, 46, 47, 50, 51, 54, 63, 67, 90, 94
    Cashew... 40, 41, 47, 53, 55, 56, 68, 69, 74, 110, 154
    Pumpkin seeds...31
    Sesame seeds... 37, 38, 90, 115, 140
    Sunflower seeds 30, 31, 40, 49, 55, 56, 57, 62, 69, 78, 82, 83, 89, 96, 97, 104, 120, 123, 141
    Walnut.. 31, 40, 47, 57, 65, 75, 99

P
Pizza Doughs..
    Basic...
        Basic Pizza Dough..14, 89, 91, 92, 93, 94, 96, 97, 99, 104, 107, 109, 110, 112, 118, 120, 121
        Pumpernickel or Rye Dough..15, 109
        Wheat and Black Bean Dough..17
        Wheat and Millet Dough...16, 119
        Whole Wheat Dough..15, 99, 102, 114, 116

    Gluten-Free...
        Buckwheat and Chickpea Flour Crust...20

Corn Polenta...17, 98
Millet polenta...18, 19, 115, 116, 159
Oat Flour Crust...21
Rice and Potato Crust...22, 122
Whole Grain Rice and Chickpea Flour...19

Pizzas...

    New World...

        Artsy Artichoke, Mushroom, and Corn...103
        Friendly Frankfurters & Kale...102
        Jumbo Gingered Gumbo...107
        Nearly Nouveaux Mex..99
        Over the Rainbow Chard...104
        Powerful Pepperoni and Mushroom..109
        Really Reubenesque..109
        Roasty Veggielicious..110
        Sausage, Broccoli, and Mushrooms...104
        Southwestern Special..99
        Terrific Tri-Pepper...106
        The Official Mad Cowboy...101
        Thymely Summer Squash...101

    Old World..

        Pizza Caponata...97
        Pizza Corn Polenta...98
        Pizza Florentine..93
        Pizza Fungi..94
        Pizza Genovese...92
        Pizza Margherita...89
        Pizza Norma..96
        Pizza Putanesca with Tempeh Anchovies..91

    Other World...

        Asian Occasion...122
        Clever Curry..119
        Gonzo Greens!..121
        Gratefully Greek..112
        Indian Samosa-Styled Pizza...118
        Krazy Kim Chi Please...115
        Pleasing Polynesian...115
        Spanakopizza..114
        St. Patty's Pizza Pie...116
        Vivid Vegetable Tarragon...120

S
Sauces...

    Basil Pesto..30, 92, 93

    Carrot Sauce...28, 59, 84

    Classic Tomato Sauce..25, 89, 91, 96, 97, 98

    Corn Comfort Sauce..36, 99

    Green Tomato Salsa...31

    Indian Spice White Sauce..35, 118, 119

    Lite Light Brown-White Sauce...33

    Mark's Mashed-Up Potatoes Sauce...36, 109, 118

    Mucho Mocko Guaco..32

    Oriental Sauce..37, 122

    Polynesian Sauce...34, 115

    Quick Italian Tomato Sauce..27

    Raw Tomato Sauce...26

    Red Tomato Salsa..27

    Rosemary Pesto...31

    Tangy Blenderized BBQ Sauce...29

    Thousand Island Dressing Sauce...30, 109

    Tofu Ricotta...34, 97

Sea Vegetables...

    Arame...92, 142

    Dulse...90, 92

    Kombu..90, 91, 92, 113, 114, 137

    Nori...90, 92

Spices..

    Caraway seeds...16, 101

    Chili powder...36, 42, 47, 58, 61, 99, 100, 107, 108

    Cinnamon...85, 135

    Cumin..................19, 27, 28, 29, 31, 32, 36, 37, 54, 55, 83, 84, 118, 119, 122, 134, 135

    Curry powder..29, 77, 84, 119, 135

    Dry mustard.......................................29, 30, 33, 50, 59, 67, 74, 80, 81, 144

    Fennel seeds..95

    Garlic powder 27, 29, 30, 31, 34, 35, 36, 47, 53, 54, 57, 62, 65, 66, 69, 70, 72, 75, 77, 80, 81, 84, 92, 93, 94, 95, 98, 102, 105, 107, 113, 118

    Ginger...29, 35, 37, 38, 52, 64, 85, 107, 108, 137

Mustard seeds..118, 144

Onion powder...27, 33, 57, 66, 69, 80, 95

Paprika.....29, 36, 42, 47, 57, 58, 61, 69, 72, 74, 79, 80, 81, 95, 100, 102, 104, 108, 109, 116, 117, 139

T

Tempeh...91, 92, 117, 142

Tofu.....1, 30, 31, 32, 33, 34, 35, 41, 44, 49, 50, 66, 77, 78, 79, 80, 81, 82, 83, 97, 102, 112, 113, 114, 115, 116, 120, 122, 138, 142, 143

Topping Sauces...

   Bean..

      Cannellini Beans, Oregano, and Walnut Sauce..75
      Chickpeas, Oats, and Pimentos Sauce..72
      Great Northern Beans, Millet, and Cashew Sauce..74
      Lima Beans, Millet, and Flax Seed Sauce 72, 103
      Navy Beans and Pecans Sauce..76
      Navy Beans, Rice, and Fresh Basil Sauce..73
      White Beans and Millet Sauce..75, 91, 115
      Yellow Dal and Rice Sauce...76

   Grain..

      Barley and Almonds Sauce...46, 94
      Barley, Carrot, and Potato Sauce 48
      Barley, Carrot, Sunflower Seeds, and Chili Garlic Sauce...49
      Barley, Cauliflower, and Vermouth Sauce...50
      Barley, Mushrooms, and Tofu Sauce...49
      Barley, White Beans, and Horseradish Sauce..47, 105, 116
      Millet, Avocado, and Oregano Sauce..51, 100
      Millet, Black-eyed Peas, and Ginger Sauce..52, 108
      Millet, Cashews, and Mustard Sauce...53
      Millet, Oats, and Cashews Sauce..53
      Millet, Quinoa, and Flax Seeds Sauce...54
      Millet, Sprouted Sunflower Seeds and Dijon Mustard...........................56, 104, 120
      Millet, Sunflower Seeds, and Oregano Sauce...55, 89, 97
      Oats, Cannellini Beans, and Garlic Sauce..58, 93
      Oats, Carrot, and Corn Sauce...59
      Oats, Cauliflower, and Carrot Sauce...59
      Oats, Mustard, and Nutritional Yeast Sauce...57
      Oats, Pinto Beans, and Salsa Sauce...60, 101
      Quinoa and Colored Sweet Peppers Sauce...64
      Quinoa, Artichoke Hearts, and Dijon Mustard Sauce...........................61, 107, 121
      Quinoa, Artichoke Hearts, and Sunflower Seeds Sauce.........................62, 100
      Quinoa, Carrots, and Corn Sauce...62

Quinoa, Cauliflower, Almonds, and Garlic Sauce..63
Quinoa, Lima Beans, and Walnuts Sauce..65
Quinoa, Sweet Potato, and Corn Sauce...65
Quinoa, Tofu, and Flax Seeds Sauce...66
Rice and Cauliflower Sauce...68
Rice and Sunflower Seeds Sauce...69, 96, 97
Rice, Cannellini Beans, and Almonds Sauce..67
Rice, Chickpeas, and Corn Sauce...70
Rice, Oats, and Cashews Sauce..68, 110
Sprouted Millet, Flax Seeds, and Cashews..55

Tofu..
Tofu and Lemon Sauce...79
Tofu and Millet Sauce...80
Tofu and Rice Sauce...80
Tofu and Sprouted Sunflower Seeds Sauce..82, 122
Tofu, Basil, and White Wine Sauce..78
Tofu, Dill, and Dijon Mustard Sauce..82
Tofu, Millet, and Cocktail Sauce Sauce..81

Vegetable..
Cauliflower, Carrots, and Black-eyed Peas Sauce..83
Cauliflower, Millet, and Carrot Sauce...84
Potato, Carrot, and Ginger Sauce..85
Sweet Potato, Oats, Carrot, and Green Chili Sauce..86

V
Vegetables..
Artichoke...41, 61, 62, 93, 94, 100, 103, 107, 112, 121, 133, 143
Arugula... 121
Avocado.. 51, 100
Broccoli..33, 101, 104, 110
Brussels sprouts... 112
Cabbage... 109, 116, 118, 137
Capers...26, 97, 104
Carrot....28, 29, 33, 40, 42, 48, 49, 51, 59, 60, 62, 63, 83, 84, 85, 86, 102, 116, 117, 118, 119, 120, 122
Cauliflower..50, 51, 59, 63, 68, 83, 84, 112, 120
Celery... 97, 106
Chard..73, 98, 104, 105, 106
Corn.......12, 17, 28, 36, 59, 60, 62, 63, 65, 70, 98, 99, 100, 102, 103, 107, 108, 123, 136
Dandelion greens.. 106

Eggplant..96, 97, 101, 107, 108, 112, 119, 123

Escarole..121

Fennel..95, 112

Garlic25, 26, 27, 28, 29, 30, 31, 32, 35, 36, 37, 38, 47, 48, 49, 50, 58, 63, 64, 67, 72, 73, 76, 78, 83, 85, 93, 94, 98, 105, 108, 110, 113, 118, 134, 137

Green beans..119

Green pepper....................................26, 27, 97, 99, 107, 108, 110, 115, 116, 120, 122

Horseradish..30, 36, 47, 62, 82, 84, 105, 116

Jalapeno..27, 31, 32, 33, 99

Kale..102, 121

Mushrooms.......24, 49, 50, 94, 95, 101, 102, 103, 104, 109, 110, 111, 114, 115, 116, 122, 140, 141

Mustard greens..106

Okra..107, 108

Olives...................................70, 85, 91, 95, 97, 100, 103, 107, 110, 112, 114, 120, 122

Onion......25, 27, 28, 29, 31, 32, 88, 91, 92, 93, 97, 98, 99, 100, 101, 102, 103, 104, 107, 108, 109, 110, 111, 112, 114, 116, 117, 118, 119, 120, 121

Parsnips..116, 117

Peas....................32, 33, 52, 70, 72, 83, 84, 108, 118, 120, 122, 134, 138, 144, 160, 161

Potato...22, 29, 34, 36, 37, 48, 65, 66, 85, 86, 92, 93, 109, 117, 118, 119, 122, 135, 136, 139, 140

Radicchio..121

Red pepper...19, 35, 101, 118, 135, 137

Romaine..121

Sauerkraut...101, 103

Scallions...38, 122, 137

Shiitake mushrooms...101, 115, 140, 141

Snow peas...116, 122

Spinach...31, 34, 50, 93, 94, 98, 100, 102, 106, 114, 121, 122

Summer squash...24, 89, 101, 102

Sweet pepper...64, 107

Sweet peppers...64

Sweet potato...29, 65, 66, 86

Tomato 3, 23, 24, 25, 26, 27, 28, 29, 30, 31, 32, 35, 82, 88, 89, 90, 91, 93, 94, 96, 97, 98, 100, 101, 102, 103, 104, 105, 106, 107, 108, 109, 110, 112, 115, 119

Turnips...116, 117

Yellow squash...19, 110

Zucchini...19, 88, 110, 119

About the Author

Mark worked at two pizza parlors out of High School and in College, and it was there that his initial interest in making pizza began. Years later, he became vegetarian, and after watching a friend make pizzas at home for a dinner party, became re-focussed on learning to do the same himself in a non-restaurant environment. After going vegan, Mark began exploring making totally plant-based pizzas. During this period he came to the conclusion that a cookbook based on these recipes would help vegetarians kick the cheese need, and vegans, who missed a good pizza, without all the fat, sodium, and animal protein.

His approach in developing these recipes changed considerably when learning of Dr. Caldwell Esselstyn's 20+ years of peer-reviewed research demonstrating that a no-added oil plant-based diet can not only reverse heart disease, but in theory, prevent it. Mark decided to incorporate this knowledge into his recipes and make them all truly "heart healthy."

Mark has been employed as the Visualizations Coordinator for two NASA Earth Satellite Missions, an interactive multimedia consultant, an organic farmer, and head photographer. He's developed media published in several major magazines and shown internationally, DVDs, websites, and managed/edited the recipes section of a cookbook. Mark has produced work for two Nobel Peace Prize winners (on global climate change) and helped in the creation & experimentation of UN Peace Medal Award-winning "birth through high school" curriculum.

Vegetarian for 20 years, and vegan for the past 11 years (over 6 of those with no added oil in his diet), he is currently the editor of the Mad Cowboy e-newsletter. An avid nature photographer, gardener, environmentalist, and an experienced and dynamic speaker/lecturer on the environment, nutrition, animal issues, and growing food, Mark can be reached at msutton@hearthealthypizza.com. *Readers of this book are encouraged to contact him with any questions, thoughts, or ideas thereof.*

Made in the USA
Monee, IL
27 November 2021